KNOW YOUR OWN SUCCESS:
Your Unique Signature

by Sharon Tobin

Copyright © 2022 Sharon Tobin

All rights reserved.

No part of this book may be reproduced in any form or by any electronic or mechanical means including information storage and retrieval systems, without permission in writing from the Publisher.

Publishers:
Inspiring Publishers
P.O. Box 159 Calwell ACT 2905, Australia.
Email: inspiringpublishers@gmail.com

National Library of Australia Cataloguing-in-Publication entry

Author: Tobin, Sharon

Title: **Know Your Own Success:** *Your Unique Signature/Sharon Tobin.*

ISBN: 978-1-922618-40-5 (Print)

ISBN: 978-1-922618-41-2 (eBook)

ISBN: 978-1-922618-42-9 (Hardcover)

'The most glorious moments in your life
are not the so-called days of success
but rather those days when, out of despair,
you feel rise in you a challenge to life,
and the promise of future accomplishments.'
— *Gustave Flaubert*

About the Author

Sharon Tobin grew up in country Victoria, where she completed her traditional education. After completing her education degree at Latrobe University, she then moved to Townsville, North Queensland with her daughter and son. Sharon further studied psychology theories and achieved her masters in guidance and counselling at James Cook University.

During her childhood and young adolescence, Sharon was exposed to the tragedy of the suicide of close family members. Now, while working within the education system, Sharon has experienced too many episodes of young adults taking their lives. This has driven Sharon to develop the 'Know Your Own Success' series of books with simple and practical activities designed as a preventative approach to suicide, rather than as a reactive approach after a failed attempt.

With 20 years' experience writing developmental courses for audiences aged between 15 and 35, Sharon has researched insight into how to assist and mentor people from diverse backgrounds and cultures.

In the past 15 years, she has also attended various coaching seminars and workshops to advance and fine-tune her personal growth, where she has developed her own style of facilitating and coaching practices to engender interest and self-confidence. Sharon has established herself as an effective presenter of meaningful content that is thought-provoking and unique to each individual's future success.

Acknowledgements

For all who have brought inspiration into my life, in your own unique way, I say thank you.

To my parents for your guiding words and actions that have forged my attitudes and values towards life from a young child until now.

To my loving partner, whose insightful truth and honesty have kept me focused.

To my darling daughter, for her astute expertise and feedback. To my son, for his level-headed view of the world.

To all who have supported my journey.

The drive in me to help others who have temporarily lost their way has been influenced by the many who have felt the impulse to inspire others. These include Albert Ellis, Albert Einstein, Albert Schweitzer, Benjamin Franklin, Benjamin Disraeli, Bernie Siegel, Charles Goodyear, David and Katheryn Geldard, Derren Brown, Dr Denis Waitley, Esther and Jerry Hicks, Henry Ford, Jim Rohn, Joe Paterno, Leonardo DaVinci, Lao Tzu, Mark Twain, Maya Angelou, Michael Jordan, Nelson Mandela, Napoleon Hill, Pamela Blewitt, Patricia Broderick, Rhonda Byrne, Robert Kiyosaki, Wayne Dyer, Wayne Gretzky, Winston Churchill, and all the anonymous greats who have also inspired many.

Dedication

This book, offered as a gift, is dedicated to all who have felt discouraged, young and old.

Foreword

Why did she do it?

In the staffroom, I processed the news from our deputy principal and felt myself go numb, remembering a similar announcement when I was 11 years old. My mum and aunty were talking quietly, weeping into tissues. I never liked it when my mother cried. I asked what had happened and they explained that their cousin had passed away. Being a curious child, I asked for more information. 'Did he have a car accident? Did he die at work?' My mum then explained that Colin had taken his own life by hanging himself. At the time I felt so angry, not because I understood what this meant, but because Colin had made my mum cry.

Now I was sitting with my fellow teachers learning about the fate of one of our students, bewildered, and asking, 'Why would she do this?' By then, I understood exactly what this announcement meant and the effect the tragic news would have on so many people for years to come.

My first cousin also took his life when I was 15, then another two cousins some years later. I have comforted friends during their time of loss and now, I work in an environment where the news of suicide seems to be the current social trend among all ages.

During my 20 years of teaching, I attended many professional development seminars about teenage suicide prevention. Each time, the presenter gave us a list of behaviours to observe that would indicate if a person was likely to attempt suicide. Upon recognising these behaviours, we would report them to the principal to investigate and then, counselling would proceed if warranted. I left each seminar with the feeling that there was a void in the available preventative measures. I also noted that the preventative measures were more of a reactive approach, taking place after a failed attempt or grievance, not before.

As the years passed and more people from all walks of life were reported as ending their lives – among them Heath Ledger, Robin Williams, Amy Winehouse, and the never-ending list of young teens – I came to realise my drive and passion were towards creating a more preventative culture for this epidemic.

Through research, observation and conversations with professionals as well as close family members and friends of suicide victims, I discovered a common behavioural characteristic. All who were associated with someone who had committed suicide would say afterwards that just before their death, they seemed ok, they seemed happy. This perplexed me. If they were happy, why would they put their family and friends through such pain? Why not suicide when they were depressed or experiencing a loss of hope? Why would they do it when they were happy?

On completion of my masters in guidance and counselling and attending various seminars, I discovered a common behavioural characteristic among successful and happy people: they all felt in control. Self-control! I then understood why it is perceived that at the very moment a person chooses to take their own life, they appear to be ok and happy. Is it because they are simply 'in control' of their own life?

With this epiphany, I began my journey towards creating the 'Know Your Own Success' book series.

Writing this first book in the series has enabled me to fulfil my vision of assisting others to become independent, self-driven and 'in control'.

Visit Sharon at:
www.knowyourownsuccess.com.au

Facebook: Sharon Tobin Know your Own Success

Or email your comments to
knowyourownsuccess@outlook.com

Contents

About the Author 5
Acknowledgements 7
Dedication 9
Foreword 10
   Why did she do it? 10
Introduction 17

PART ONE: Know Yourself 19
Week 1 21
   Strengths and Weaknesses 21
   Discussion 22
   Individual Activity 23
   Weekly Task 24
Week 2 25
   Who Do You Want to Be? 25
   Individual Activity 26
   What Do You Want to Do? 26
   Discussion 27
   Vision Board 28
   Weekly Task 29
Week 3 30
   What is Holding You Back? 30
   Discussion 30

Individual Activity 31
Who is Holding You Back? 32
Weekly Task 34
Week 4 35
   It is OK to Brag 35
   Discussion 36
   Counting the Wins 36
   Individual Activity 38
   Weekly Task 39
Week 5 41
   Unlearning to Learn More 41
   Discussion 42
   Individual Activity 43
   Weekly Task 44
Week 6 46
   Changing Attitudes 46
   Individual Activity 48
   Discussion 49
   Shifting Your Thinking 50
   Weekly Task 53
Week 7 54
   Your Ideal Future 54
   Discussion 55

Individual Activity 56
Vision Board Review 57
Weekly Task 58
Week 8 59
Influences in Your Life 59
Discussion 60
How People Perceive You 61
Individual Activity 62
Weekly Task 63
Week 9 64
How You Perceive Yourself 64
Individual Activity 65
Adopting a New Posture 65
Discussion 66
Weekly Task 68

PART TWO:
Know Your Intention 69
Week 10 70
What is Your Intention? 70
Discussion 72
What are Your Habits? 72
Individual Activity 73
Weekly Task 74
Week 11 75
What are Your Values 75
Discussion 76

Individual Activity 77
Weekly Task 79
Week 12 80
Types of Decisions 80
Discussion 81
Genuine Decisions 82
Individual Activity 83
Half-Hearted Decisions 84
Weekly Task 85
Week 13 86
Challenging vs Safe Decisions ... 86
Discussion 87
Reckless Decisions vs
Challenging Decisions 87
Individual Activity 88
Weekly Task 90
Week 14 91
Decision-Making Strategies 91
Discussion 91
Observation 92
Individual Activity 94
Gathering Information 94
Weekly Task 96
Week 15 97
Narrow Your Options 97
Discussion 98
Individual Activity 99

Correcting Your Course............100
Weekly Task 101

Week 16 .... **102**
Deciding or Wishing....................102
Individual Activity 103
What Brings You Joy 104
Discussion..104
Weekly Task 106

Week 17................................. **107**
Setting a Goal................................... 107
Discussion..108
Individual Activity 109
Weekly Task 111

Week 18 .... **112**
Your Responsibility to You 112
Discussion.. 113
Individual Activity 113
Weekly Task 115

PART THREE:
Know Your Own Success............ **116**

Week 19 .... **117**
Act or be Acted Upon...................117
Discussion..117
Individual Activity 119
Weekly Task 120

Week 20 .... **121**
Procrastination..................................121
Discussion..121
Being Assertive................................123
Individual Activity 124
Weekly Task 125

Week 21................................. **126**
Feeling Out of Control 126
Discussion..127
Individual Activity 128
Feeling in Control 129
Weekly Task 131

Week 22 .... **132**
Overcoming Fear 132
Discussion.. 133
Individual Activity 133
Strategies 134
Weekly Task 139

Week 23... **141**
Temporary Setbacks 141
Discussion..144
Troubleshooting..............................144
Individual Activity 145
Weekly Task 146

Week 24 .... **147**
   Action with Purpose 147
   Discussion 147
   Action with Passion 149
   Individual Activity 150
   Weekly Task 152

Week 25 .... **153**
   Taking Responsibility 153
   Discussion 153
   Individual Activity 155
   Reaching Your Goal 155
   Weekly Task 157

Week 26 .... **158**
   The Perfection Myth 158
   Discussion 158
   What Success Means to You 160
   Individual Activity 162
   Weekly Task 163

Week 27 .... **165**
   Believe It Will Be 165
   Discussion 165
   Things Happen for a Reason 166
   Individual Activity 167
   Weekly Task 167

Week 28 .... **169**
   The Ideal You 169
   Weekly Task 171

Epilogue 173
References 175

Introduction

If you asked the question, 'What do I need to do and have to live my life successfully?' you could not sum up your answer by considering only one aspect of your life to guarantee overall success. Your life is made up of both complex and simple pieces of a puzzle. Every piece of the puzzle represents a different area of your life, including career and employment, lifestyle, finance, love and romance, and family. Your individual puzzle is very different from anyone else's. It is unique.

Everyone is unique in their own right. With every thought you have, every decision you make and every action you take, you are inscribing your Unique Signature onto the world and it looks very different from everyone else's. Your Unique Signature is one of a kind and is made up of your personality, the inner you. This 'you', while affected by many outside influences, guides you to achieve what you want in life. Consider a chef and their 'signature dish'. Over many years of trying different flavours and discovering new recipes, they then choose what flavours appeal to them and create their signature dish. Your Unique Signature also changes over time. Think about your official signature and what it originally looked like when you first inscribed it. It would look very different now. Your Unique Signature on life changes with every experience you encounter.

What you are about to commence is a course of simple, practical activities and tasks to develop your Unique Signature in all areas of your life. They are a collection of effective self-guided activities and tasks that only apply to *your* individual needs and wants. As you work through completing the course, it is highly recommended that you keep legible notes to refer to, while completing additional activities and tasks.

Every Discussion, Individual Activity, andWeekly Task has been developed by using Research and Reflective Practices, following the Psychology theories of Humanistic and Existential, Positive Psychology, and Rational Emotive Behavioural and Cognitive Therapy.

In Part One, you will 'Know Yourself' and discover, or rediscover, what your ideal Unique Signature looks like to *you*, now and in the future. In Part Two, you will 'Know Your Intention' and gain a clear perspective of the accomplishments you want in your life. In Part Three, you will expand your confidence and 'Know Your Own Success' to become the person *you* want to be. The complete course is essential for all pieces of the puzzle to fit comfortably into all aspects of your life.

> **'Whatever the mind can conceive,
> it can achieve.'**
> — Napoleon Hill

Part One: Know Yourself

'Knowing Yourself' is understanding that your biggest asset in achieving your ideal life is your mind. Any idea begins with a thought. With that thought a plan is created. That plan is then put into action. Your mind controls all these processes to make that idea become a reality. We all have the power to think big, but only some of us have the belief that our ideas are possible and the determination to make them happen. Our success in life also depends on what we think of ourselves and whether we believe in our abilities to succeed.

What if we could change our life with a single thought? With every life event, we experience a range of emotions, both positive and negative. Reacting with emotion sometimes creates undesirable outcomes. What if we could experience everyday situations with better results by adopting a different reaction to these situations?

By implementing proven strategies that will develop our objectives in life, we will be able to enhance our accomplishments, our sense of wellbeing and our self-confidence to influence our ideal Unique Signature and our destiny in life.

What are your thought, For they become words?

What are your words, for they become actions?

What are your actions, for they become habits?

What are your habits, for they become you character?

And what is your character, for it becomes your destiny?

What we think we become.'

— Unknown

Week 1

Strengths and Weaknesses

Strengths and weaknesses mean very different things to different people. What is ideal for one person is not necessarily ideal for the next. One person's strength can be another's weakness.

An example would be to compare a social worker and a police officer, both professions serving the public. For a social worker to be effective in their position, they need to be empathetic towards the person they are working with. Having empathy enables a social worker to establish trust with their client. This is a strength. However, if a police officer demonstrated empathy while making an arrest, it could result in a very serious situation, which would be a weakness for the officer. The strength of an officer is in being assertive and upholding the law.

Our strengths and weaknesses are part of our Unique Signature. They are what make us who we are at certain stages of our life. Our Unique Signature changes every day. Every time we experience something in our life, positive or negative, it creates a weakness or a strength and changes our Unique Signature. Because we are learning new things every day, some weaknesses can be temporary, meaning we haven't yet achieved and mastered the strengths we are seeking.

Remember when you were a child first learning to tie your shoelace? Once you learned this skill, the experience made you more independent and gave you strength. Before learning this skill, you depended on others (parents, siblings, family friends) and it was a weakness. Now you take this learned knowledge and strength for granted.

Discussion

Think of one significant thing you learned this week.

Were you seeking to gain a strength from this newly learned knowledge?

Is this newly learned knowledge something you can use to your advantage?

There are many situations throughout our lives where we will experience weaknesses, and that's ok. This does not make our life any less or more valued than anyone else's. People will always be at different stages in their life. Some know less than we do, and some know more. No matter how minute your knowledge or ability may seem to you, it's what makes you, you. So it's ok to have weaknesses. Without them we would not strive to learn and achieve new experiences or abilities and turn them into strengths.

Sometimes we push certain weaknesses aside because we are too embarrassed to admit we have them, or we don't know how to overcome them. We live in a society that is very age orientated about knowledge. At this age we should know this, and at that age we should know better, and so on. This unrealistic pressure, very evident within our schooling system, can result in feelings of self-doubt and low self-esteem. Just because you may not know something that someone else knows does not make you less knowledgeable or valued. It is guaranteed that you know something or have a particular skill that someone else doesn't.

Reflect again on the example of the social worker and the police officer. Both occupations are equally important, and each has specific knowledge and skills they utilise to their advantage. This is also evident between a tradesperson and a musician, who have different knowledge and skills and serve society in their own unique way.

Individual Activity

List five things you see as your strengths (e.g. problem solving, talking to people, self-motivated, musical ability, sports, caring for siblings).

At what age were you aware you had these strengths?

Are there some people in your life who do not have these strengths?

Are you able to assist others who do not have the same strengths as you?

How does it make you feel when you're able to help others using your strengths?

The best way to strengthen any weakness we may have is by being self-aware.

To know our strengths and weaknesses is to learn and grow, to determine what is important to us, and to create the Unique Signature we are seeking that feels right to us.

Weekly Task

Choose a weakness you are aware of.

Consider the strengths you already have that could help you overcome this weakness.

During this week, focus every day on overcoming this weakness. This may require learning a new skill. Remember, new skills mean new strengths.

Who could you help by using your newly discovered strength?

Each week from now, try to overcome small weaknesses that may be holding you back.

'To know our strengths and weaknesses means we are being accountable for our thoughts, our words, our actions, our accomplishments and our dreams.

All are a part of our Unique Signature.'

— S.T.

Week 2

Who Do You Want to Be?

In all aspects of our life, we are naturally making decisions about 'who we want to be'. This, in turn, affects our Unique Signature at any particular time in our life. How we make decisions and cope with different situations depend on our strengths and weaknesses. For example, it is human nature to display either 'engagement' or 'avoidance' behaviours, such as engaging in situations we believe in or choosing to 'avoid' them.

Depending on what is important to us, at a particular time in our life, not all situations need to be engaged in. Take two people who want to skydive, for example. One wants to be a skydiving instructor and the other just wants to experience the thrill of the jump. Now let's say that both people are petrified of heights. The question is to 'leap or not to leap'; 'engage' or 'avoid' the situation. The person who wants to jump for the thrill of it has no personal investment in whether they jump or not. Therefore, if they back out of the jump it just means they don't experience the thrill and in the scheme of their life experience, it probably isn't very important to them. However, the person who wants to become a skydiving instructor has a personal investment in engaging in the situation. Taking a stand and doing the jump is very important to them.

Individual Activity

List three situations where you have demonstrated engagement behaviour.

List three situations where you have demonstrated avoidance behaviour.

How did each situation represent the person you want to be?

Be aware of why you may decide to 'leap or not to leap', 'engage or avoid'. This self-awareness can assist you in achieving the strength you seek to become the person you want to be, your ideal Unique Signature.

What Do You Want to Do?

When we are young, most of us have an idea of what we want to do when we grow up. Some people may not know until they are much older. Someone who thinks about doing fire-fighting at the age of five may then decide to do administration duties when they are venturing into the workforce at the age of 16, then later realise their passion for running their own business.

Whereas some people will be satisfied doing one thing for the rest of their life, other people will want to do many different things. In turn, some people will be satisfied to live in one location for their entire life, while other people will want to live in many different locations.

Discussion

What did you want to do when you were younger (tradesperson, teacher, truck driver, parent)? Have these goals changed?

Will you need to learn new skills to achieve what you want to do?

What strengths and abilities do you currently have that will help you achieve them?

Many factors in our life determine what we want to do, including influences of family and friends, commitments imposed by family as well as self-imposed commitments, formal education, self-education, strengths and weaknesses.

All these factors play a very big part in what we are able to achieve at different stages of our life. For example, your parents may own a family business selling computer equipment. Due to this influence, you may be very knowledgeable about computers, and working in this industry may be your first job. You may also have a passion for looking after animals and through self-education, you study all there is to know about training dogs so that after a while, you are able to start working at a dog shelter or veterinarian clinic.

If you then decide to do medicine but have no prior knowledge or formal education within this area, you will need to invest in yourself and have the commitment to overcome this lack of knowledge and skills to achieve your new goals in life.

> **'Formal education will make you a living,
> Self-education will make you a fortune.'**
> — Jim Rohn

Everything we do makes up our Unique Signature in life. We all have the ability to change who we are and what we want to do to become who we want to be at any stage of our life.

Are you happy with your current Unique Signature?

Vision Board

A vision board is a visual tool used to inspire and remind us of what we want in our life. It is a representation of our current Unique Signature and what we want our Unique Signature to be in the future.

Your vision board could be made up of pictures of what you want and what you have already achieved, personal inspirational words, positive affirmations and quotes, or a combination. The purpose of your vision board is to acknowledge what you have already accomplished and inspire what *you* want your Unique Signature to look like. To inspire you to be the person you want to be.

Weekly Task

List what you want in your life and who you want to be (material items, house, car, dream job or career, holidays).

List accomplishments you have achieved and the strengths you have to support what you want next.

Every day this week collect pictures, quotes, affirmations, and personal words that have inspired you so far, and will inspire you to achieve your goals in life.

Arrange your collection of inspirations and display them somewhere in your home so you will view it, every day.

Every time you view your vision board, say to yourself, 'This is my life and my Unique Signature' – and most importantly, believe it.

Week 3

What is Holding You Back?

Once you have decided what you want to do and who you want to be, think about what is holding you back.

Creating a vision board is only the beginning of creating our ideal life. Our vision board represents the proof of the accomplishments we have already achieved and the belief we hold within ourselves of what we are capable of achieving next. However, if we don't believe in ourselves, nothing we want will become a reality.

Discussion

Reflect on all the things you have achieved in your life so far.

Did these achievements happen by chance or did you truly want them to happen?

Would these achievements have happened if you hadn't believed they could have?

Think of a time in your life when you really wanted something to happen. All your energy and enthusiasm were directed towards this and it somehow seemed to happen by magic, with everything falling into place with ease. Now think of something else you wanted but your energy and enthusiasm weren't fully directed towards it happening and it occurred with great difficulty or not at all. There are two main reasons why things we want don't happen. One reason is that it wasn't a priority for us at that particular time in our life. The other reason is we didn't believe we could achieve it.

Our lack of self-belief in our abilities is one factor that can hold us back from achieving what we want and who we want to be. We can have an idea, but if don't believe we can, then that idea won't become a reality. An idea is only a dream without self-belief.

So why is it we sometimes don't believe in ourselves? Fear, lack of motivation, different priorities, weaknesses? All these factors have something in common – you. You are the one who can overcome your fear, get motivated, change your priorities, and overcome your weaknesses. It's all up to you, and only you. You are the first step towards creating your Unique Signature and the life you want.

Individual Activity

Consider one thing you could have achieved in your life and haven't yet.

Why haven't you achieved this yet?

Is this achievement important to you or is it just a whimsical dream?

Would you be willing to overcome what is holding you back for this achievement to become a reality?

Can you use any of your current strengths to make this achievement happen now?

Be aware of *not* being your biggest weakness. Try not to procrastinate about achieving what you want. There are two major reasons why we procrastinate about a situation. The first is fear: we are scared of creating something different in our life, or afraid of the reaction of the people closest to us. The second reason is that we don't really want this something in our life. This tends to happen if we are achieving something for someone else and not for ourselves.

As mentioned earlier, if achieving something is not important to you at a particular time in your life, it's ok not to achieve it now. However, if you are not actively achieving the things you want for yourself, you may become disheartened about who you truly *are* and want to *be*.

Who is Holding You Back?

Sometimes we make excuses about why we haven't achieved something in our life. Why not just be honest with ourselves and say to others, 'That wasn't important to me at the time'? It's because many of us value what people think of us, especially when the people are close family members, friends and who we look up to.

When our closest family members or friends voice their opinion about what we have or haven't achieved in our life because it differs from their expectations of us, we may doubt our strengths, abilities and the Unique Signature we want at a particular time in our life.

Let's revisit our example of the family computer business, from Week 2. It could be an expectation of the parents that their child will continue with the family business after completing their formal education. Their child may then decide to continue the family business only because it's what their parents expected of them and not because they really wanted to. The decision made by this person could be solely influenced by them not wanting to disappoint their parents. With this decision made, is the person being true to their inner self? Are they truly strengthening their Unique Signature with the positive attributes they want in life?

Are you currently achieving something in your life for someone else's motive and not your own? It's ok to live part of our life according to others' expectations. In a functioning society we are expected to act in a certain manner in order to respect the law and those around us. We just need to be cautious about living our entire life as a reflection of what others want of us and remember to be true to ourselves about what *we* want in life. If we live our life so far removed from what we truly want, we tend to feel unhappy and not in control. This lack of control can lead to low self-esteem and have very negative effects on our wellbeing.

'You have the absolute authority within you to make your own choices.'
—Book of Revelation

Weekly Task

If you haven't already, share your vision board with a close family member or friend.

Tell them with conviction, 'This is my life and my Unique Signature', and most importantly, believe it.

Explain to them what your Unique Signature looks like to you.

If they seem interested, invite them to create their own vision board.

If they create a vision board of their own, make time each week to discuss any achievements you have both accomplished in your quest towards your ideal Unique Signature.

Along your new journey it is important to identify with the people who are going to carry you forward in a positive way. If you experience a negative reaction from someone close to you about your vision board, that's ok. It just means they're not ready to let go of the 'old you'. People like familiarity in their surroundings and the people they interact with, making them feel comfortable in knowing and predicting situations to come. Changing any aspect about yourself can make some people uneasy when they are used to you acting in a certain manner.

It's ok to agree to disagree when interacting with other people in different areas of your life. Show them your new strength and how you can support them in their life's journey.

Week 4

It is OK to Brag

Everyone, some time in their life, has experienced an obnoxious person who continually brags about *everything*. Let's have a look at why. The person may just be obnoxious, or they may have another strategy that works for them. Expressing to the world what we have achieved boosts our self-confidence and self-belief. Some people *can* go over the top, but remember, it's ok to agree to disagree with other people's Unique Signature.

To achieve anything we want in our life and to boost our Unique Signature, we must have a desire. All desires begin with a thought, and what we think we become. Bragging affects the way we think and feel about a situation, how we view ourselves, the people we interact with, and our environment. If we think positively and feel positive, we tend to brag more. Therefore, to be the person we want to become, it's ok to brag. Bragging can be an effective strategy to kick-start our mind into thinking positive thoughts.

There are many ways to brag. If you have participated in the weekly tasks so far, you have already started to brag. By telling yourself, 'This is my life and my unique signature', you are bragging. By creating your vision board and sharing it with someone close to you, you are bragging. Your next brag will be telling yourself aloud, 'I will achieve…'

Other ways of bragging might be to invite family and friends around to have a look at a new addition to your home; have a party to celebrate a special occasion; invite your vision board buddy to help celebrate a win; or even more daring, stand in front of the mirror every morning and tell yourself how great you are and what you will accomplish that day. Whatever form of bragging comes naturally to you, do it with pride.

Discussion

Think of one thing you can brag about right now. How does this thought of bragging make you feel?

If you feel comfortable, yell it out to the world.

If you don't feel comfortable about doing that, write it in CAPITAL LETTERS and place it on your vision board.

Congratulations on a brag well done, because it's ok to brag.

Counting the Wins

Counting the wins is simply about acknowledging the achievements we have accomplished so far. It's about knowing that the next achievement is possible because we have done it before. It's about acknowledging that something we thought could not be done, has been done because we made it happen. Remember riding a bike for the first time? Counting the wins is, most importantly, about being proud of our strengths, our ability, our confidence, and what lies ahead in creating our ideal Unique Signature on the world.

When we set a goal, it is important to remember to celebrate the small wins along the way. If we wait and only celebrate the final win after accomplishing the big picture, we can become overwhelmed and give up on ourselves. We need to feed our self-belief with tangible possibilities. Small steps at a time and celebrations will in turn lead to bigger wins.

Take our skydiver wanting to be a skydiving instructor, from Week 2. Every step along the way to accomplishing this grand vision is a win that should be celebrated. When they book the plane for their first jump, when they complete their first jump, when they enrol in an instructor's course, when they pass their first exam, and so on. All of these wins will keep them enthusiastic about the next step and focused and motivated towards their final goal and greatest win.

When we count the small wins, we need to be aware of how they make us feel. When we feel good about ourselves, we are able to see clearly opportunities that present themselves and accomplish more of what we want, easily. This will be explained further in the weeks to come.

Individual Activity

Tell someone about three things you want to achieve this week (think of some small wins for the week, they don't need to be big).

Explain in three words how you believe these wins will make you feel.

Will these wins assist your ideal Unique Signature?

What new strengths will you gain from these wins?

Be aware of how long it took before you celebrated each win. Some wins will happen quicker than others. If a win took an unreasonably long time to occur, ask yourself, 'Did I really want this win to happen?' and 'Did I stop this win from happening earlier because of fear?' If you answered 'yes' to either of these questions, a self-evaluation is important for moving forward with a positive mindset. Don't be negative about failing to accomplish a win. Self-evaluation and being aware of our conscious effort helps us learn about what we truly want and becomes an internal guide. Just remember, everything will eventually fall into place and our greater wins will be realised.

If fear is holding you back, searching for a way to overcome this next time will turn another weakness into a strength you can utilise later on. The strategies described in Week 22 will assist in overcoming a range of fears.

Weekly Task

Display on your vision board the three wins you want to achieve this week.

Read them aloud, with conviction: 'I will achieve...' and most importantly, believe you will.

Explain to yourself how these wins will be in alignment with your Unique Signature.

Discuss your wins with your vision board buddy or a close family member or friend and embrace the enthusiasm and drive this gives you.

Once you have achieved each of these three wins, reward yourself. For example, treat yourself to something you would not normally do or have.

Make it your mission to achieve these three small wins this week. Believe in your abilities and the strengths you already have to accomplish these wins.

To remain true to our ideal Unique Signature, it is important to be accountable for what we say we will do. If we truly want something, we will find a way to engage and make it happen.

Every time we achieve something new and count our wins, we strengthen and enhance our Unique Signature to become the person we want to be. Over time, our Unique Signature is filled with many inspiring abilities, including independence, confidence, certainty, courage, and tenacity, to name a few.

> **'Stand tall, walk straight,
> fear no one's thoughts or words.
> Be proud of being you.'**
>
> — S.T.

Week 5

Unlearning to Learn More

Unlearning is all about opening our mind to bigger and better opportunities. It's about acknowledging that our previous Unique Signature would have been adequate for when we were younger, but that our Unique Signature now needs to develop and take on new transformations as we enter new phases of our life.

For example, when we were very young, we opened our mind to the possibility of walking, then running and eventually, riding a bike and climbing trees. As an adolescent, we may have opened our mind to more adventurous activities that represented our Unique Signature at that stage of our life, such as writing stories, rock climbing or driving a car. As we get older, we tend to open our mind even more and explore the possibilities of skydiving, bungy jumping, buying a house, opening a business, joining the defence force, or flying a plane.

In each example, from one stage in our life to the next, from one strength to a greater strength, from one Unique Signature to an improved Unique Signature, we unlearn what we *once* thought was possible and learn what *is* possible at this stage of our life.

When we learn something new, we naturally link it to our already established knowledge and experience, which is the foundation for learning more exciting things in our life. We must first learn how to walk before we can run. However, this already established knowledge and experience can sometimes cloud our confidence and have a negative impact on our ability to achieve something new.

Remember our skydiver. We are taught at a young age, through the experience of falling over, that when we hit the ground it hurts. To complete the act of skydiving, we must unlearn the possibility of hitting the ground and be open to the possibility of the experience of floating on a pocket of air, landing safely on the ground, unharmed.

Discussion

Reflect on something you have achieved by using the foundation of your prior knowledge and experience.

Did you believe you could achieve this with ease?

Now think of something you have wanted to achieve in your life but haven't.

Is the reason for not achieving this new experience due to having certain prior knowledge and experiences causing you to doubt your abilities?

We have all been conditioned to think a certain way. Some conditioning is designed to protect us, such as laws and safety regulations. But much of the conditioning we experience is someone, or ourselves, conditioning us to believe 'we can't because...' This may create negative values in our life, such as, 'I will never be good enough'.

This 'because' may make sense at the time; however, later on we may realise that the 'because' was only a way of keeping us from escaping a familiar setting. This familiar setting may be our family and friends, our place of employment, our residence and geographical location. If we challenge this familiar setting, we open our mind to possibilities without limitation as to what we can achieve.

> 'Learning never exhausts the mind.'
> — Leonardo DaVinci

Individual Activity

Think of one thing you want to do that is outside of your familiar setting.

How does the thought of changing this familiar setting make you feel?

Is this change worth enough to you to engage?

What would you have to unlearn to make this change happen?

To unlearn something is to move away from and let go of the idea of what's 'not possible' and look at the idea of what 'is possible'. People who actively look for new opportunities are those who are constantly unlearning and changing their Unique Signature to suit the life they want for themselves. All these people have one thing in common: they have learned how to break free from conditioning limitations.

Have you heard about the tale of the elephant? When an elephant is a young calf, keepers chain it to a stake in the ground that can withstand the calf's weight of 100 kgs. No matter how hard the calf tugs on the stake, it will not break free. As the calf develops into a fully grown 6,800kg elephant, it is conditioned to staying chained to the tiny stake. Even though the size of the stake hasn't changed, the elephant will not tug on it due to its prior experience of not being able to escape.

> **'If you accept the expectations of others,
> especially the negative ones,
> then you will never change the outcome.'**
> — Michael Jordan

The process of removing the limitations that blind us to greater opportunities includes questioning our classical conditioning, identifying and discarding negative values and repeatedly focusing our awareness on our ideal Unique Signature.

Weekly Task

Examine your vision board and identify what your future Unique Signature looks like.

Identify and list any foundation or life skills you would consider as strengths in working towards your unique Signature.

Now identify and list any limitations and negative values you may have that need to be unlearned.

Describe how unlearning these limitations will strengthen your ability to create a new setting for your future Unique Signature.

Discuss your new setting(s) with your vision board buddy or a close family member or friend.

Remember, the person you discuss this with may not agree with the idea of you changing any of your familiar settings. They may be hesitant to discuss this matter with the 'new you' and try to maintain the 'old you'.

To stay confident with unlearning and overcoming our limitations, we must be aware of changing opportunities and believe in our ability to adapt to these experiences and situations that suit our desired lifestyle, which is essential for us to thrive in the different stages of our life.

Week 6

Changing Attitudes

Everything you have read so far and all the activities you have participated in for the past five weeks have been designed to embrace the mindset you require to accomplish the Unique Signature you are seeking and the lifestyle you want.

Overcoming 'weaknesses' and transforming them into 'strengths' is a major factor in becoming *confident* in dealing with challenges we face in everyday life. Creating a vision board is a major factor in *believing* what we are capable of accomplishing in our life. Identifying 'what is holding us back' and 'who is holding us back' are major factors in *problem solving*, to become *independent* and take *ownership* of our desired life. 'Counting the wins' and 'bragging' about our achievements are major factors in remaining *true to ourselves* for what *we* want out of life. 'Unlearning' our limitations is a major factor in *opening our mind* to all the possibilities and opportunities that surround us daily.

The words above that are *italicised* are major indicators of the kinds of attitudes we need to adopt to be successful in creating our desired Unique Signature. *Confident, believing, problem solving, independent, ownership, true to ourselves* and *opening our mind* are all essential ingredients for changing our attitude.

'If we don't change anything, nothing changes.'
— S.T.

Many experts say that to succeed in anything requires a combination of attitude and ability. Most people think it is important to first have the ability to be able to achieve something. If you think back to Week 1, 'Strengths and Weaknesses', it was suggested that 'a weakness is only a strength that we haven't yet mastered'. To master a strength, overcome a weakness and turn that weakness into an ability, we must first have the attitude of wanting to overcome the weakness. Therefore, it is not important to first have the ability in order to achieve success in most parts of our life.

Attitude is everything. We either have the attitude towards succeeding or the attitude towards failing. If we do not have the attitude to succeed in what we want, our self-belief will become low and our confidence will diminish in that area of our life. Think back to riding a bike for the first time. Did you believe you could ride it (attitude of success) or that you couldn't (attitude of failure)?

Also, when learning a new ability, we must sometimes unlearn our limitations and the only way to do this is to have the correct attitude and be open-minded towards achieving it.

Individual Activity

Write down three tasks you have attempted but didn't really want to do.

Write down three tasks you have attempted that you wanted to do.

Considering both scenarios:

Which tasks were you determined to achieve?

Which tasks did you give up on halfway?

Which tasks did you find easy to complete?

Which tasks did you find difficult to complete?

If our attitude is not 'in it' 100%, we tend to struggle to complete the task or complete it at a much lower standard. Therefore, completing the task correctly then requires an even longer commitment.

So if we have no interest in achieving something and our attitude towards that something is very low, why should we even bother? At one time or another, we all experience situations where we don't *want* to do something, such as studying for an exam, mowing the lawn, filing paperwork, and so on. But if we focus on the big picture of what we are trying to accomplish, then completing the task makes sense.

Think back to our 'engage' or 'avoid' scenario and what is or is not important to us. We need to be aware that if we skip a step along the way because we couldn't be bothered, it may jeopardise our ideal future Unique Signature, or delay what's possible in the next stage of our life.

Discussion

Consider baking a cake. The ingredients are simple: flour, sugar, eggs, milk, and flavouring.

Let's say you only have half the ingredients and you need to drive to the local supermarket to get the rest, but you can't be bothered.

Is it possible to make the cake without all the ingredients?

Could you use different ingredients to achieve the same result?

Will the cake taste the same?

Life experiences are similar. If we don't have all the ingredients to achieve a major aspect of our life, we may find ourselves achieving a different result than the one we originally set out to accomplish. This in turn will produce a different Unique Signature.

Think about the ingredients for buying a house. You first need a deposit or some sort of equity before you can obtain a home loan. Now let's say you have managed to save $30,000 meticulously over the past three years and are only $10,000 away from achieving the deposit you need to secure your dream home.

Along comes a close friend and prompts you into taking a trip around the world. If you choose to go with the friend, your Unique Signature of owning your own home has now been delayed.

This scenario can also happen the other way. What if your Unique Signature was to use the $30,000 to travel around the world for a year, then you meet someone special, settle down and use that money as a home deposit instead?

There is no right or wrong way in either scenario. Each scenario is unique to the individual and if we are *true to ourselves*, whatever we want will fall into place because we have chosen for it to happen that way. We are the absolute authority for what happens and what doesn't happen in our life.

It's your Unique Signature; *you* choose.

Shifting Your Thinking

You've heard of the saying 'the glass is half empty or half full' or 'can't see the forest for the trees'. Both represent how people view their environment and their current situation. People who see the glass as 'half empty' are said to have a mindset of not seeing opportunities when they arise; and the people who see the glass as 'half full' are said to have the mindset of seeing opportunities. Likewise, people who only see the trees are said to dwell on problems, while people who see the forest are said to have the ability to problem-solve to achieve the big picture.

The above does not sum up any one person. We all experience different situations in different ways, and act differently in different situations. For example, a person could have a very good sense of direction and the ability to navigate road maps. If they were to find themselves lost in the city, they would not have any difficulties problem-solving to find their desired location. They would be 'seeing the forest through the trees'. However, this same person could experience a bad situation with someone in their life and have no idea how to resolve the problem. They might think, 'what's the point, nothing will change'. This person who is great at problem solving with navigation adopts a negative mindset when dealing with a different situation and seeing the glass as 'half empty'.

As mentioned earlier, our weaknesses and strengths determine how we experience different situations and problems that may arise, no matter how large or small. Our prior experiences, our weaknesses, our strengths, our habits, and also our attitude to unlearning limitations and learning new skills, determine if we experience the same problem over and over again or overcome them.

**'The definition of insanity is doing the same thing over and over again but expecting different results.'
— attributed to Albert Einstein**

Over the past three weeks, you have been asked to discuss your vision board with a close family member or friend.

How has this task been going for you?

Have you been comfortable about discussing your ideal Unique Signature?

If not, could changing your mindset develop this weakness into a strength?

Have you found any adversities when discussing your ideal Unique Signature?

If so, did you continue to engage in the belief of your future; or did you choose to avoid the conversation and surrender the idea of the 'new you' for the sake of keeping the peace?

These questions might be a bit challenging. However, they are necessary to shift your thinking in order to experience success in multiple areas of your life; rather than living a life that may feel comfortable and easy, that is dominated by the decisions and opinions of others. By asking yourself these types of questions, you are evaluating who you are today and who you will be tomorrow.

Remember, your ideal Unique Signature is your future and who you are striving to become. At no stage should you abandon this vision just because someone close to you does not agree. Every time you abandon your vision, you are in danger of becoming very far removed from who *you* really are. And *you* are worth fighting for, every minute of every day to become your ideal Unique Signature.

Weekly Task

Reflect on when a conversation about your ideal Unique Signature was changed or ignored due to a disagreement or a misunderstanding with a close family member or friend.

Consider your attitude towards the conversation and how it made you feel. (It's a natural response to feel angry, upset or frustrated.)

Afterwards, could you see a resolution or have you chosen to dismiss talking about your Unique Signature with this person ever again?

Your task this week is to re-establish the conversation about your Unique Signature with the same person.

Write down what you could have done or said differently to change the outcome of the conversation.

If you find it a bit difficult to talk about this again, write a letter to that person explaining why this is important to you.

The most important step in this week's task is to shift your thinking and change how you would normally approach a problem to discover a way to 'see the forest through the trees'. Remember to keep a firm grip on your ultimate prize, the ideal *YOU*.

Week 7

Your Ideal Future

We have many potential futures in our lives, where endless possibilities are available every minute of the day. They can also change from one day to the next. With everything we learn, with every weakness we overcome, with every strength and ability we gain, with every problem we face, and with every changed attitude and mindset we choose, we are altering our future. Simply stated, our ideal future is what *we* want it to be.

What this means is that at any stage of our life we are able to change our future, and our current circumstances are *only* our current reality. Most thoughts we have about our future are in response to what we are observing right now. If we see ourselves not being successful in one area of our life, we have a very unrealistic view that our future will remain the same as it is today. If this was a true representation of our actual reality, we would have never learned how to walk, run or ride a bike.

The reality is that every opportunity is an opportunity to learn. It depends on whether we take that opportunity and make it our own. If we choose not to take an opportunity now, there will always be time to reconsider that opportunity later in life. For example, if a person does not attend university at the end of their formal education, they could easily attend university as a mature-aged student when the time is right for them.

'You create your own universe as you go along.'
— Winston Churchill

Time is a man-made concept and we are not necessarily restricted to time when it comes to achieving new abilities. Humans in general tend to place an expectation of time on when we should know something. However, many of us develop at different stages and it also depends on what's important to us at that particular time of our life and what we want our Unique Signature to look like now and in the future.

Discussion

Think of something you had the opportunity to achieve when you were younger but chose not to pursue it.

Did you reconsider this opportunity later on? If not, would it be important for you to do so now?

If you did achieve this later on in life, was accomplishing this opportunity easier than expected?

Think about the shift in your thinking that enabled you to move forward in achieving this opportunity.

Was this accomplishment in alignment with your ideal Unique Signature?

As we get older, we look at our past through different eyes. In doing this, we sometimes stand in judgement about what we have and haven't achieved. Some people even go so far as to call their past a 'misspent youth'. This implies that some of what we accomplished as a youth was a waste of time. Our youth is anything but a waste of time. They are the most impressionable years of our life in shaping our idea of what we want our future Unique Signature to look like.

Individual Activity

Write down three things that you have accomplished as a youth (or that you accomplished in your youth).

What strengths and abilities have these accomplishments given you?

Write down three things you enjoy(ed) doing as a youth.

Can you link each enjoyment to your accomplishments?

Everything we achieve as a youth is the very foundation of the person we become. In history, there have always been improvements made to human creations. The vehicles we drive today are well advanced from Carl Benz's first concept of a gasoline car; high-rise buildings that we occupy today are well advanced from the basic dwellings of the past. All foundations are made to be built upon and all are influenced by experiences of the past. Your Unique Signature is no exception. It is your grand creation, made up of the foundations and improvements *you* have decided for your ideal future.

Vision Board Review

In Week 2, you were asked to create a vision board to represent your current and ideal future Unique Signature. You were also asked to place the vision board in an area of your home where you could view it every day. When you viewed it, you would recite to yourself, 'This is my life and my Unique Signature', and most importantly, believe it.

Believing this mantra when you say it is a form of visualisation. Daily visualisation creates a shift in our thinking that is required for our ideal Unique Signature to take form. There are many ways to visualise. You could sit quietly while seeing what you want in your mind and feeling joyful about having it, you could meditate or you could stand in front of a mirror and view your reflection as having what you want. It is more personalised when you choose what best suits you.

Visualising has been clinically proven to stimulate the areas of the brain that are responsible for opening the mind to see opportunities when they arise. Dr Denis Waitley (1986) conducted a study with a group of Olympic track athletes who were connected to high-tech biofeedback equipment where they were asked to run their event only in their mind. Muscle stimulation in their brain was activated in the same way as if they were physically running the event. The brain could not distinguish between the athletes imagining or physically running their event. This is known as visual motor rehearsal (muscle memory).

Simple examples of muscle memory are writing your name, or changing gears in a car without looking. Once this muscle memory has been established, we never forget how to do it, just like riding a bike. The more we participate in visualising what we want, the more our muscle memory expects it to happen for us right now. Therefore, it is important to visualise what we want in the present tense. For example, 'I am a design engineer', rather than, 'I will be a design engineer'. If we only think of what we want in the future, it will always remain in the future.

> 'Tomorrow never happens;
> it is forever tomorrow.'
>
> — S.T.

Weekly Task

Revise your aspirations on your vision board. After five weeks of unlearning and learning activities, do you still want the same things and the same goals?

If not, change or add to your vision board. Remember – it is your life, so it's ok to fine-tune what you want and who you want to be.

If you are happy with your goals, rearrange your collection of aspirations and prioritise them.

Every time you view your vision board, say to yourself, 'This is my life and my Unique Signature', and most importantly, visualise it as being now.

Week 8

Influences in Your Life

The influences in our life vary according to where we live, where we work or study and what we do during our recreational time. However, the greatest influence in our lives are the people we interact with.

> **'We are the company we keep.'**
> — Unknown

The above saying refers to our mannerisms and the attitudes we adopt when we are influenced by the people we interact with. Not only do we act in a certain manner, we also adopt a certain frame of mind when interacting with different people in our life. If we are subjected to pessimistic and negative opinions about the world and ourselves, we tend to adopt a generally negative attitude to our life. On the other hand, if we are subjected to optimistic and positive opinions about the world and ourselves, we tend to adopt a generally more positive attitude towards our life.

People who are influenced by positive people are generally happy about themselves and their life. If a person walks into a room smiling, they have a more positive effect on the people around them than a person who looks gloomy. And whether we realise it or not, we have a huge influence on the people around us. For example, if someone around you is smiling and having fun, it's natural to smile as well. This is then passed on from you to the next person you interact with.

This domino effect occurs when we are influenced by what the people we admire the most say or do. As young children we would naturally mimic the people we look up to. As an adolescent or adult, this is no different.

Discussion

Think of someone you admire.

What is it about them you admire?

Do they have a positive outlook on the world?

Do they display strengths and abilities in their life you would like to adopt as your own?

Is there anything they do or say that you sometimes imitate?

When being influenced by people, it is a responsibility to ourselves to be accountable for what we want and who we want to be. This might be feeling good about a situation we experience as confirmation that we are in alignment with our Unique Signature. However, if we are influenced by something or someone in a particular situation that makes us feel uncomfortable and far removed from who we want to be, we have the authority to remove ourselves from that situation and seek a more deserving experience.

We cannot always control a situation, but we can control how we experience a situation. Simply removing ourselves from an uncomfortable situation or conversation can protect our wellbeing and create the strength of independence and maturity. If we continually ask ourselves, 'Is this what I want my Unique Signature to feel like?' and follow this self-guidance, we are guaranteed to achieve what we are seeking.

How People Perceive You

There was once an old lady who lived in a well-to-do country town where wealthy people retired. This lady would wear dresses that were stained and had rips in them, shoes that were too big and when she spoke, her false teeth would fall out of her mouth. Once a week, she would walk around the local football oval and collect scraps from the rubbish bin to feed her scruffy looking dog. What is your impression about this lady – do you think she is successful or not?

She gave a first impression that she lived in poverty and that she struggled financially. However, she was one of the wealthiest people in the town and gave generously to charities and people in need.

Our attire gives the first impression of how people perceive us, well before we open our mouths to talk or before we do anything. If we present with torn and dirty clothing, it may be perceived that we are not serious about achieving our future successes. If on the other hand we present in neat attire, this is generally perceived to mean that we are very serious about our future and that we are driven to succeed.

Our attire is like the cover of a book. When choosing a book or magazine from a store, we choose the one that looks the newest and with pages that are not dog-eared. It may be harsh, but the reality of society is no different from this analogy. Several 'make-over' television shows illustrate this. Respected, successful people dress well. They are admired on the red carpet around the world.

When we establish ourselves in a certain area of society, it is our responsibility to dress accordingly. This prompts respect from others as well as self-respect. Think about the very first time you attended an important interview or function. The type of clothing you chose would have reflected what was appropriate to that particular setting. Would you attend a job interview in your singlet and thongs, or a school formal in your school gym uniform?

When we wear something that is clean and well presented, it gives us confidence and we feel good about ourselves. Improving our attire is one way that can help us feel positive about who we are. Also, wearing the type of clothing that represents our ideal Unique Signature could help us adopt the mindset we require to accomplish what we want.

Individual Activity

List what you normally wear around your home.

Is this attire different from what you wear outside your home?

List the attire you would wear if you were attending a very important interview or function.

How do you feel when you are well dressed and you see your reflection in the mirror?

Weekly Task

Think of someone you admire, whether they are famous or not.

Do they represent what your Unique Signature looks like?

List the type of clothing they wear.

Every morning when you look in the mirror, imagine yourself wearing that type of clothing.

Say to yourself, 'This is my life and my Unique Signature', and most importantly, visualise actually wearing the clothing now.

If possible, go shopping and find the attire you have been visualising.

When you wear your new attire, tell people 'this is the new me'.

Remember that if anyone questions the 'new you', engage with them confidently. Be what and who you want to be and don't change your attire back into the 'old you' just because someone may not agree. It's ok to agree to disagree.

Week 9

How You Perceive Yourself

How we perceive ourselves is usually very different from how people perceive us. How people perceive us is dominated by external expressions (what we look like). How we perceive ourselves is formed from self-image and internal expressions (how we feel).

Over the past eight weeks, you have been completing individual activities and weekly tasks that include overcoming weaknesses to create strengths and new abilities; creating a vision board and reflecting upon it; identifying what and who are holding you back; counting your wins and bragging; learning how to unlearn to create a productive attitude and mindset; and identifying influences on you and the influences you have on other people. All these activities and tasks have been designed to make you aware of how you perceive and feel about yourself and the accomplishments you have already achieved in different aspects of your life.

Think back to just before you had accomplished something. If you perceived yourself as achieving this, you would have found the task easy to accomplish. However, if you had told yourself, 'It'll never happen to me', then it most probably didn't, or it was extremely difficult for you to accomplish. When we perceive that we can accomplish something, we feel good about what is happening in our life. In turn, this reflects on what we look like, which has an impact on how people perceive us (the cover of a book). Does the way you perceive yourself at this moment reflect your ideal Unique Signature?

'Perceive yourself as successful and you will be.'
— S.T.

Individual Activity

When you are happy about an accomplishment, be aware of what you look like.

Look at your facial expression, your body language and your posture in the mirror.

Be aware of how people interact with you. Be aware of what influence you have on them when you are feeling happy.

When you are feeling happy, take note of how you perceive yourself at that moment.

Using a moment of accomplishment can help us perceive ourselves in a positive way. If we are feeling good about how we perceive ourselves, we are in alignment with our ideal Unique Signature.

Adopting a New Posture

A person's posture says a lot about them. Their body language also shows how they truly feel about themselves. When a person is self-assured, they stand tall with their shoulders back, hold their head up with pride and have a bounce in their step when they walk. On the contrary, when a person is not self-assured, they slump their shoulders, drop their head and walk with heavy steps.

The person who walks into a room smiling would stand tall, have their shoulders back, hold their head up with pride, and have a bounce in their step as they walk. Their posture radiates confidence and certainty, they are remembered and people aspire to become like them.

Discussion

Consider someone you know who is generally less confident about their life.

What is their posture like? Which attributes mentioned do they display?

Consider someone you know who is generally confident about their life.

What is their posture like? Which attributes mentioned do they display?

Think of a person you admire. What are their attributes and posture? Do they radiate confidence and certainty?

So how do *we* adopt a particular posture that radiates confidence and certainty? When we have accomplished something and overcome a weakness to create a strength and a new ability, it makes us feel positive and happy about ourselves. This then reflects in our body language and our posture, and helps us become accustomed to having a confident and radiant posture. Once we are aware of this, it is easy to adopt this posture more frequently.

Thinking about people having an influence on how we experience different situations and how we also have an influence on other people, our contributions towards a conversation or atmosphere can simply alter depending on the posture we adopt. let's think back to our skydiver. The skydiver would naturally find the experience jubilant if everyone around them was supportive and excited. More so, the posture of the skydiver would display certainty for what they were about to do. To the contrary, would they feel positive about the jump if the people around them showed negative emotions?

In order for our ideal Unique Signature to become a reality, it is vital for us to be aware of our posture. By simply asking, 'Does this posture reflect my ideal Unique Signature?' it is possible to prompt ourselves back into alignment with what we are seeking. If the answer is 'no', then take time to reflect on how it could be better aligned. Remember to allow time for these developments to happen naturally. If we reflect every time we view our vision board, we can ascertain how closely in alignment we are with our ideal Unique Signature and adopt the relevant posture we desire.

Weekly Task

Reflect on the following questions and write a list of all the things that have changed and how they have changed over the past eight weeks.

What new strengths and abilities have I developed?

Am I still holding myself back?

What wins have I bragged about? Do I feel confident enough to brag?

How have I been influencing the people around me?

How has my attire changed? How do I now perceive myself?

Am I adopting the posture I require for my ideal Unique Signature?

Answering all these questions honestly will give you a true picture of how you have developed in the past weeks to create the ideal Unique Signature you desire. If you feel there are some areas that are not quite in alignment, revisit each activity and weekly task and complete them again. Remember, this is your life. Taking extra time to achieve what you want and who you want to be is your absolute right.

> 'We shall act with good intentions,
> but at times we will be wrong.
> When we are, let us admit it and try to right
> the situation.'
>
> — Joe Paterno

Part Two: Know Your Intention

'Knowing your intention' is about understanding the purpose for achieving anything you want. Your values determine your intentions towards your ideas and thoughts, plans and actions. This in turn determines your overall success in achieving your ideal life.

What if we could change our habits by changing our intentions? Every life event we experience, positive or negative, reflects on our intention to succeed. If our intentions to succeed are not in alignment with our ideal Unique Signature, we can sometimes create undesirable outcomes.

What if you could experience everyday situations with better results by adopting a different approach to how you apply your intentions?

By implementing proven strategies that help achieve our life objectives, we enhance our accomplishments and our sense of wellbeing and self-confidence, influencing our ideal Unique Signature and our destiny in life.

The 'Knowing Yourself' activities are closely connected to those for 'Knowing Your Intention'; every intention we have reflects on who we are. The decisions we make also deeply reflect who we are and who we want to be, which have a huge impact on all stages of our life.

Week 10

What is Your Intention?

Knowing what we want and who we want to be is a major influence in what our intentions are. If we have a weakness, is it our intention to transform it into a strength? If we hold ourselves back, or someone else does, is it our intention to pursue what we want? If we accomplish something great, is it our intention to count the win? And to look the part of our ideal Unique Signature, is it our intention to adopt a suitable posture and body language that reflects this?

To be true to ourselves and to create an atmosphere of trust with the people we interact with, it is essential to reveal our intentions. This does not mean making an announcement to the world with every decision we make, but presenting our posture and body language that represents who we truly are.

When a person's intention is hidden, different severities to a situation can emerge. Think of a child who intends to snatch a piece of food from the family fridge after their parents have said 'no' due to dinner being served shortly. The child will do their utmost to hide their intention so they don't get caught (we have all done this). This example would create a minor consequence to the overall integrity and interactions of the household. However, if we think about the intentions of a conman or woman, the consequences of hiding their intentions could be dire for the people they interact with.

'Our intention creates reality.'
— Wayne Dyer

In some circumstances, our intentions may affect people in a way we may not have originally intended. For example, refer back to the person who works in the family computer business. If it is their intention to leave the family business to pursue their dream of working in medicine, out of respect for their parents, they should reveal their intention of eventually leaving the family business. The parents may not agree with them, however, if their intention is shared, this creates trust and understanding between the parents and their offspring.

In this example and many other circumstances, it may be awkward to discuss your intentions with close family members or friends, due to not wanting to hurt their feelings or alter their expectation of you. However, the overall outcome would be more positive than not sharing your intentions at all.

Discussion

Think of someone you have interacted with who tends to hide their intentions.

Think of someone you have interacted with who naturally reveals their intentions.

For each scenario:

Which person do you feel relaxed and comfortable around?

Which person would you tend to be cautious with while interacting with them?

Do you sometimes hide your intentions from other people?

How do you think this makes them feel around you?

What are Your Habits?

Remember that with every thought we create, we also create an intention, which in turn reflects our habits.

What we have completed over the past nine weeks has been designed to focus on new intentions and creating new habits, while being less influenced by old intentions and habits that have not been productive towards our ideal Unique Signature. Be aware that there may be times when we feel discouraged about what we are yet to accomplish and resort to displaying old intentions and habits that serve no purpose. Keep in mind that when our intentions and habits are in line with our Unique Signature, we feel good about what we are doing and who we are. These feel-good emotions let us know whether we are on track or not. The better we feel, the more in alignment we are. Conversely, the worse we feel, the more out of alignment we are. If our intentions and attitude are in line with our ideal Unique Signature, our habits will be also.

Individual Activity

Consider something on your vision board that you have accomplished in the past nine weeks and note down:

How did accomplishing this make you feel?

Did this accomplishment create a new habit?

Thinking about your feelings of accomplishment, do they inspire you to complete other aspirations from your vision board?

Has there been a time over the past nine weeks where you have fallen back into old habits?

If so, are these habits in alignment with your ideal Unique Signature?

It is very easy to unconsciously do things that bring out automatic behaviours of the 'old you'. For example, if a person who is saving for their dream car has an old habit of spending their entire income every week, they will find it very difficult to save until this habit is broken and the habit of saving their income is established.

With every intention to achieve something, we must stay focused on the intention of creating new habits for our new achievement to become a reality.

Weekly Task

For this task, refer back to Week 9's Weekly Task.

Look over the list you created about all the things you have changed over the eight weeks prior.

Next to each item on your list, write down your intention for changing what you have changed. State 'my intention is to...'

It is important for each intention on your list to be very specific. Stating 'to create my ideal Unique Signature' is too broad.

Next to each item on your list, write down any habits you have changed in order for each intention to become a reality. State 'my new habit is...'

For example:

Change Made	My Intention is to	My New Habit is
Smile at people	Make them and me feel happy	Hold my head up with pride
Not giving up	Succeed in what I want	Persistence and engaged behaviour

Discuss your list of intentions and new habits with your vision board buddy. Ask if your intentions and new habits have been evident. Ask your buddy for some productive feedback. However, you need to ensure you are ready to receive this feedback. Remember it's ok to agree to disagree.

Week 11

What are Your Values

When people talk about values, they are referring to what is most important to them. Our values are personal and determine how and what we do in our life.

In Week 1, we explored our weaknesses and strengths and chose to overcome the weaknesses by the values we keep. As presented in Week 2, we identified what we believed was worth engaging in, in light of our values. We also discovered that an achievement that is important to one person may not be important to another. Achievements are also driven by our values and they can look very different to different people.

For example, one parent could devote their life to getting up early each morning to make their children's lunches because they place a high value on assisting their children and giving them a good start in the morning. Another parent may insist their children make their own lunch as their most important value could be developing their child's independence. Neither parent loves their child any less than the other and each child would have the innate understanding that their parents have the best intentions for them.

Our values may also change in different situations and be challenged in challenging situations. Let's take a look at the value of being truthful. Everyone wants to perceive themselves as honest and they expect the people they interact with to also be honest. However, if one day a police officer was to book you for speeding, would you correct the officer and admit you were actually going five kilometres faster than what they stated on the ticket? Or would a child admit to eating the last choc-chip cookie when they weren't allowed to? Self-preservation makes us reluctant to dob ourselves in.

Discussion

If a person who valued being truthful told a little white lie to someone because they didn't want to hurt their feelings or get into trouble, would this diminish their values?

Think of a time when one of your values has been challenged. Did this alter the way you viewed having this value?

The reason for telling a little white lie may not have a great effect on our overall values. However, we may experience other challenges that do. As our values are greatly influenced by our experiences as well as by the people we interact with (parents, close family members and friends), we may often feel that our values are being challenged more often than not.

Let's revisit our person working in the computer shop. Does this person hold the same values as their parents? When they announce to their parents they are leaving the family business to start a different career, they may find this situation very challenging. The values instilled in them by their parents would be naturally tested, such as the obligation of 'family stick together' or 'the family business should be passed on to a family member' or 'this is the way we've done it for generations'. It is in our nature to want to please the ones who are an important part of our life.

In some circumstances, a compromise could be a solution. For example, they could offer to work in the family business on weekends. When we face these challenging situations, we must remain true to ourselves and ask 'is this what my Unique Signature looks like at this particular time in my life?'

Individual Activity

While completing this activity, you may decide to visit a website listing a range of different values. Simply Google - 'list of values'.

List ten values you personally hold close to your heart (e.g. integrity, generosity, knowledge, punctuality, empathy, cleanliness).

Who or what influenced these values?

If you had to give up one of these values, which one would it be?

What was your reasoning for letting go of that value and not another?

How did this make you feel – was it a struggle to let one go?

If you did not find it difficult to give up one of your values, this could indicate that the value may not be in line with your Unique Signature.

Spend some time going deeper to discover what values are most important to you. There are websites that list over 400 values that could help you explore your true values.

> **'The major value in life is not what you get.
> The major value in life is what you become.'**
> — Jim Rohn

Having the values that feel natural to us are important in forming our ideal Unique Signature. They help us make appropriate decisions and navigate difficult terrain in our life. Sometimes our values can easily become misguided as a result of the interactions and influences we have from other people, such as someone close to us voicing their opinion or disapproval. This may cause a challenge to establish our values and find the strength to change our habits to reflect them.

In Week 5, we discussed the idea of unlearning old habits and opening our mind to learning new habits that would assist us in creating our ideal Unique Signature. Which habits we decided to change would have been influenced by the values we hold in high regard. We may believe in a value but sometimes our habits may not reflect this. Examples might be spending money when we are planning to save, watching endless hours of television when we are wanting to lose weight, not studying when we are expecting to pass an important exam. Our values determine our intentions that, in turn, become our habits and if these are not in alignment, we must either change our habits or decide that this particular value is not what we are seeking for our Unique Signature at this time in our life.

Weekly Task

Consider five of your top values.

Now think about an average day, week, month in your life, the things you do and how you spend your time.

Do your habits reflect your values?

Beside each value write how your habits are meeting or not meeting your values.

Choose the value that you regard the highest. Over the next week, plan to be authentic to this value, every day.

At the end of the week, reflect on how this made you feel.

In the following weeks, concentrate on being true to another of your top five values (reflect on one each week).

While completing this task, if a value feels good and right to you, hold on to it and enjoy the experience. If it doesn't feel right, it's ok to let it go. Ensure you are choosing the values that are right for you and that reflect your ideal Unique Signature.

Week 12

Types of Decisions

Have you ever experienced a situation where you should have made a different choice? Some people live their lives full of regret and some with no regret at all. Being regretful about a decision indicates we are not in alignment with our true self.

In Week 2, we explored the idea of engagement or avoidance behaviours and reflected on which best represented our true self, as we delved into the possibilities of taking on different opportunities throughout our life. In completing each weekly activity, we can also conclude it is never too late to change our mind or our pathway to achieve who we want to be and what we want out of life. Therefore, feeling regretful about a decision is only relative to a specific time in our life.

Let's reflect on our skydiver who wants to be a skydiving instructor. They have decided to overcome their fear of heights to make this happen. Before this decision, they may have regretted never taking to the sky, then after the experience it is no longer a regret. Remember, in our lifetime, we continually make choices we feel are right at that particular time in our life.

'Don't regret, just do it when it's right!'

— S.T.

How we feel about the decisions we make is our natural guidance system letting us know whether something is what we want or don't want. It's important to feel good about the choices we make. If we are aware of not feeling good or even becoming desensitised to a situation, we are protecting ourselves against what we don't want. We need to make the appropriate adjustments towards what we do want. If any choice causes us to experience regret, it is our responsibility to revisit this decision and make it right.

Discussion

Reflect on a time when you have felt excited about making a decision (buying a new gadget, going on a holiday, starting a new job, choosing a new area to study).

Did this decision feel right to you?

Did you want to share this decision with someone?

Did you feel any regret after making this decision?

Did you feel this decision was in alignment with your Unique Signature at that time in your life?

In Week 4, we talked about 'Counting Our Wins'. Our wins are a direct result of the decisions we make. Start with small decisions to create smalls wins. If we set out to accomplish something that is too big, we may become overwhelmed and give up on ourselves. Remember, we need to feed our self-belief with tangible decisions that reflect tangible wins. Making small decisions naturally leads to bigger, more confident decisions and the bigger wins that will follow.

During this and the coming weeks, we identify four different decision types that most people are accustomed to making. Reflecting on these types of decisions can help us accomplish our ideal Unique Signature sooner rather than later.

Genuine Decisions

Most genuine decisions are made when we are feeling good about ourselves. We see things around us more clearly than when we are stressed.

In Week 6, we viewed the concept of seeing the glass half full versus seeing it half empty, and seeing the forest through the trees versus seeing the trees through the forest. When we are stressed about a situation, we focus only on the problem at hand and view the glass as half empty, or focus on one tree at a time, not the entire forest or possible outcome. Focusing only on the problem can cloud any obvious solution that may be presented to us.

Also, when we are stressed, interactions with other people and the things around us don't run smoothly. Little problems seem bigger and careen out of control, making our daily routine daunting and giving us the feeling of a heavy load on our shoulders, which is reflected in our physical posture. If a situation or lifestyle choice causes us elevated stress levels, this is our internal guidance system telling us we are not in alignment with our ideal Unique Signature. The clouding effect, provoked by stress, also means we are not making our decisions confidently. In turn, we may lose our stamina or frequently change our mind about what we want.

When making a genuine decision, we tend to focus on the outcome, not the problems that may arise, and so we maintain a strong, healthy belief that what we are doing is right. We rarely deviate from the decision we have made and we engage to make it happen, no matter what it takes. When making a genuine decision, we view the glass as half full and we see the entire forest, not the individual trees. We make the decision with confidence and self-belief. We feel happy, contented and excited about the outcome being successful. Our drive creates an unstoppable force where the outcome will naturally fall into place and feel right for what we want and who we want to be. This feeling tells us we are in alignment with our ideal Unique Signature.

Individual Activity

List five decisions you have made in the last month, big or small (applying for a job, going to a party, buying a car).

For each decision, note the following:

Did you make each decision when you were stressed or clear-minded?

Did you really want to make each decision?

How did each decision make you feel?

Did you achieve the outcome you were looking for?

Can you identify which decisions were genuine decisions?

Did any decision alter your attitude or values in any way?

Half-Hearted Decisions

We make half-hearted decisions when we are not 100% sure of what we want, not confident in our ability to accomplish what we want, or the decision is what someone else wants.

We sometimes make decisions that are influenced by other people. Some of these decisions are in line with our Unique Signature and we feel good about the outcome. However, the decisions that are not in line with our Unique Signature are generally approached half-heartedly and a successful outcome may take longer or not at all. In making these decisions, we are sometimes placing other peoples' wants in front of our own needs and rewards. This is not to say that we shouldn't compromise with others or deliberately create situations of unnecessary hostility. This statement is about being true to ourselves and our ideal Unique Signature.

Making half-hearted decisions also depends on our strengths and weaknesses. If we are confident about accomplishing something, our focus becomes very driven towards that outcome. However, if we feel we have a weakness in a certain area of our life, we tend to adopt a half-hearted attitude towards the desired outcome. This way we are protecting our emotions and dignity by telling others, 'I didn't really want that anyway', rather than admitting to ourselves we failed due to a weakness we had not previously overcome. An example would be our skydiver refusing to jump because of fear, then telling others it wasn't important. Once again, to minimise experiences of regret from the decisions we make, ascertaining what is important to us at that time in our life and choosing to overcome a challenge or walk away from it ensures we are in alignment with our ideal Unique Signature.

'If we want it, we will find a way!'

— S.T.

Weekly Task

List some half-hearted decisions you have made in your life.

Were these decisions based on your idea or someone else's?

How do you feel about these decisions now? Regretful or not?

Examine your vision board and decide if any of your half-hearted decisions from the past are now worth accomplishing, and are in alignment with your ideal Unique Signature.

Over the next week, decide which aspirations on your vision board will prevail as genuine decisions within your ideal future, or whether they are half-hearted decisions.

Week 13

Challenging vs Safe Decisions

As mentioned earlier, when we feel confident about our ability to accomplish something, our decision is focused and we are driven towards the outcome. Decisions made when we feel certain about succeeding are called 'safe decisions'. Safe decisions are acceptable if they are in alignment with our Unique Signature. However, if they are made due to fear of stepping outside our comfort zone, safe decisions can potentially create a false sense of security and we may constantly experience undesired circumstances in our life. By continually only making safe decisions, we limit our potential to overcome weaknesses, unlearn conditioning beliefs, learn new abilities, and open our minds to new and exciting opportunities.

Challenging decisions are a healthy way to develop into our ideal Unique Signature. They are where our learning commences and enthusiasm for life is created. Think about the skydiver and the person from the computer shop. A safe decision would be for the skydiver to choose not to jump and let the opportunity of becoming a skydiving instructor remain a dream; or the person chooses to work in their parents' computer shop for the rest of their life instead of pursuing their vision of becoming something they desire. When the skydiver chooses to jump, or the person informs their parents of their intention, they open up new and exciting opportunities, stepping outside their comfort zones to learn new strengths and abilities they will carry forward with momentum and enthusiasm for life.

Do your decisions challenge and inspire you? Or are you playing it safe?

Discussion

Think of a decision you have made recently.

Did you make this decision because it was safe or because it would challenge your abilities?

If you made a safe decision this time, think of the last time you made a challenging decision.

Reckless Decisions vs Challenging Decisions

Reckless decisions can sometimes be mistaken for challenging decisions. We generally make reckless decisions when we are avoiding facing the responsibilities of previous decisions. For example, if our person from the computer shop left the family business to study a medical profession to fulfil their goal, this would be a challenging decision reflecting their move towards their ideal Unique Signature. However, if they then decided to quit medicine due to the exams becoming too difficult, this decision would be a reckless one that would have detrimental effects on achieving their ideal Unique Signature, and it might result in future regrets.

Most reckless decisions are made due to the influence of other people, or from fear or a lack of confidence or self-belief. When we are certain about what we want and who we want to be, our decisions start to reflect this and consequently, we make fewer reckless decisions and more challenging decisions with greater confidence and self-belief.

We make challenging decisions when we have the confidence to know we are accomplishing something that will move us towards who we want to be. If we are not sure where to begin when making a decision that will improve our life, it may seem reckless to step out of a comfort zone we have become accustomed to. However, making a challenging decision is when we expand our knowledge, our abilities, our intentions, and our values in line with achieving our ideal Unique Signature.

Individual Activity

Look at your list of the five decisions from last week's individual activity.

For each decision, note the following:

Do you feel each decision was moving towards your ideal Unique Signature, or moving away from it?

Determine if each decision made was a safe, challenging or reckless decision.

Which decisions were you genuine or half-hearted about?

After the outcome of each decision, can you see yourself being closer or further away from your ideal Unique Signature?

If we continually make reckless decisions, we tend to adopt a half-hearted attitude towards our life. Because we are not experiencing positive results or progressing, we start to believe that we have been a failure in everything we have done. This lack of self-value makes us vulnerable and very far removed from who we want to be; and has very negative` effects on our wellbeing. Remember from our Week 1 task, things we consider to be failures are simply temporary setbacks or weaknesses, which can easily become strengths.

Without failures or weaknesses, we would not strive to create positive abilities that move us towards the life that feels right for us. Every failure we experience may be perceived as a reckless decision at the time, however, it creates a positive opportunity to learn from our mistakes, which is a very healthy part of life. The feeling of failure is one of our internal guidance systems that lets us know when we are not in line with our Unique Signature. We need to make adjustments in order to succeed. It is only when we choose to let failures dominate our values and choices that they become an unhealthy part of our lives. The reality is we will never experience success without first experiencing failure.

'The measure of success is not whether you have a tough problem to deal with, but whether it is the same problem you had last year.'
— John Foster Dulles

Weekly Task

List some failed decisions in your life (e.g. education, work, career, relationships, travel, residence).

State why you believe these are failures (only your part in them, not someone else's).

What positive outcomes or different direction in your life did these failures create?

How do you feel about these failures now?

Over the next week decide if any of these failed decisions:

Are temporary setbacks or weaknesses you are now ready to turn into strengths and abilities?

Were reckless decisions?

Were challenging decisions that will move you towards your Unique Signature?

After completing this task, take note to realise there are actually no life-long failures. A failure is simply an indication of being on the wrong path towards our Unique Signature, or an indication that a part of our life needs to be strengthened in order to fulfil our Unique Signature. Our feelings will indicate which is correct.

Week 14

Decision-Making Strategies

Whether we decide to act or not to act, both are decisions. Every decision we make is a reflection of our intentions; our intention to do something or not to do something. With every intention, we create a plan. This plan is not always presented on paper. Most of our plans are simply our thoughts about what we are going to do next. Whether we succeed or not has a huge connection to whether we planned a decision or if we just 'went with the flow'.

> 'If you fail to plan, you plan to fail.'
> — Benjamin Franklin

Discussion

Look at your vision board. How do you plan to succeed becoming your ideal Unique Signature?

Think about how you have planned in the past.

Do you only plan in your head what's going to happen next?

Do you write your plan out on paper and tick off each task when completed?

Do you go with the flow while other people make decisions for you?

Have these strategies been successful for you in the past?

Over the next two weeks, we will concentrate on decision-making strategies that are designed to enhance our ability to plan the steps needed to succeed in becoming our ideal Unique Signature.

Observation

Is there such a thing as luck? Are there naturally lucky people in the world? Are you one of these lucky people? Do you believe you are unlucky?

Some people we have interactions with seem very lucky. They have their ideal career, their ideal house, their ideal car, their ideal... Are these people lucky, or did they plan for their ideal life? If we state and believe 'that only happened to them because they were lucky', it generally means we didn't see the same opportunity. A study conducted in 2011 by Derren Brown, *The Secret of Luck*, found that people who consciously observed opportunities typically found luck. As part of the experiment, a 50-dollar note was placed on the footpath in the pathway of a man who described himself as 'unlucky'. He walked directly over the note and failed to observe it being there for the taking. When asked why he didn't pick up the money, he replied, 'I didn't see it'. Throughout this study and many other social studies, it has been demonstrated that only a small percentage of people observe and take the opportunities presented to them, while a larger percentage of people fail to see any opportunities at all.

Observation is the first and most important strategy when making a decision to improve our life. Without observing opportunities when they present themselves, there is a big chance they will slip by without us even noticing. If we adopt the attitude that 'only good things happen to other people', we are setting ourselves up to continually miss observing the exact opportunity we may be waiting for. Some opportunities are even missed because of fear, or because we do not believe in ourselves. In Week 6, we talked about the types of attributes for adopting the correct mindset to successfully experience what we are seeking (*confidence, self-belief, problem solving, independence, ownership, true to ourselves* and *opening our mind*). Adopting these attributes will assist our habit of naturally observing and embracing the opportunities that will create our ideal Unique Signature.

Opportunities can also be missed due to the influence of peoples' opinions about certain opportunities. In Week 3, we discussed achieving something in our life for someone else and not our own. This may also contribute to our failure to observe obvious opportunities. People's expectations of us can sometimes cloud our judgement as to what opportunities are best for us. Remember, it's ok to take a moment to reflect on what we truly want for ourselves; and it's ok to share our intentions about the opportunities we want to observe and pursue, even if they may not agree.

Individual Activity

Consider a time when you missed an opportunity (study, work, travel, buying a car or a house, a relationship).

What caused you to miss this opportunity? Because you didn't see it, because of fear or because of someone else's opinion?

Has this opportunity presented itself since?

Is it possible for you to recreate the opportunity you missed?

Has this missed opportunity delayed achieving your ideal Unique Signature?

When an opportunity passes, we may need to wait until it presents itself again. This could be a matter of hours, days, weeks, or sometimes even years. We may become disheartened by having to wait, or we could try to create the opportunity for ourselves.

> **'One secret of success in life is for a person to be ready for an opportunity when it comes.'**
> **— Benjamin Disraeli**

Gathering Information

Once we have observed an opportunity, the next step is to gather information about it and assess how it will affect our overall plan towards achieving our desired outcome. This is conducting due diligence, which and is a form of self-education, arming ourselves with the important information that will determine if the opportunity aligns with our ideal Unique Signature.

For example, if we observed an opportunity to study overseas in a foreign country, we would need to educate ourselves on their local language, the currency they use, what accommodation is available, what internet providers there are, whether we can afford to go straight away or if we need to budget, what responsibilities we may be abandoning, and most importantly, whether the opportunity serves our intentions for becoming who we want to be.

Opportunities presented by family members or close friends may include their opinions and advice, such as, 'That's what I did when I was your age'. An example of this is when buying a car, where family members or close friends convince us it's a great deal. In this situation it is more necessary than ever to do our own 'homework', as we can sometimes blindly trust the people we are close to without questioning if it is right for us. Conducting our own due diligence means deciding for ourselves if this is a reliable purchase. Do I need to spend extra money to fix it up? What are the extra costs involved to maintain the vehicle? Can I afford the loan repayments? How long will it take to make the final payment?

'Care and diligence bring luck.'
— Thomas Fuller

Some opportunities may look very exciting and promise the world. However, if we jump into an opportunity without knowing what we need to succeed, or if it is to our benefit, we may find ourselves giving up halfway. The result of not gathering the right information can lead to making half-hearted decisions and wasting time and resources, which may be more detrimental to our Unique Signature as opposed to not seeing the opportunity at all.

With every decision we make and every opportunity we embrace, there may be either positive or negative consequences. Experiencing positive consequences is a fundamental step towards knowing that our intentions and values are in alignment with our Unique Signature. Feelings of happiness and self-satisfaction arise from gathering the right information and making informed decisions. If we are anxious or uneasy about a decision, that tells us we need to gather additional information before making any further decisions on this matter. Information and knowledge create certainty and wisdom.

Weekly Task

List some opportunities you have let slip by in your life (e.g. education, work, career, relationships, travel, residence).

Have you considered why you have not accomplished these opportunities in the past?

Does this opportunity appear on your vision board?

During the next week, gather all the information you need in order to make an informed decision about an opportunity you want to pursue now (cost, time, availability, responsibilities, skills needed, support network, material resources).

Week 15

Narrow Your Options

At a young age, we may have some idea of what we want to be when we grow up. However, as soon as we become of age, it does not mean we will automatically achieve this goal. There are likely to be other achievements in our life that we will need to accomplish before this goal becomes a reality for us, such as attending a certified course and completing prerequisites before advancing further, or moving locations to where the opportunity is offered.

Each opportunity we observe is accompanied by many variations as to how to achieve the outcome we seek. Sometimes the most direct pathway may not be the best. Whether we take a direct or a roundabout route towards achieving an opportunity depends on what our strengths and abilities are and how soon we plan to achieve the opportunity.

> **'The most successful route will be the one you chose yourself!'**
>
> — S.T.

Discussion

Referring to last week's Weekly Task and the information you gathered, how many different pathways have been presented for you to pursue each opportunity?

Have you observed these pathways in your life before?

At this stage in your life, which pathway appeals to you the most?

Narrowing our options for a desired opportunity is a simple strategy to use when deciding the best pathway to take, after we have collected all relevant information and completed our due diligence. We can take the following steps to narrow down our options and eliminate any doubts, fears or uncertainty about what we truly want.

Step 1: Determining what needs to be unlearned

This is the most important step. Our learned, limited beliefs can cloud what we are capable of achieving and hold us back from deciding on an appropriate option. When we adopt the correct mindset of 'believing we will succeed' and implement an 'open-minded attitude', we have a clearer vision of which opportunities will create the success we are seeking.

Step 2: Reflecting on our current abilities

This is essential for overcoming our weaknesses and undertaking self-education in a particular area before we can proceed with an opportunity. A challenging opportunity may allow us to discover a new strength we didn't realise we had and the ability to notice further opportunities.

Step 3: Establishing what our intentions are

We need to ensure our intentions are in line with our current or future ideal Unique Signature. Some opportunities we face meet our established knowledge and strengths, which may make the decision look very appealing and safe. However, if an opportunity is not in alignment with what we visualise our ideal Unique Signature to be at this particular stage or for the future, it may prove to be a time waster and serve no purpose.

Step 4: Finalising outstanding obligations and responsibilities

This is vital when moving towards the next opportunity. If we leave an area of our life unfinished, it may result in future regrets, the creation of bad habits (flitting from one opportunity to another) and a lack of intention and values towards attaining our ideal Unique Signature.

Individual Activity

Considering the four steps above to narrowing your options:

Are there any steps you are familiar with?

Are there any steps that created a 'light-bulb' moment?

Reflect on how reading each step makes you feel.

Does any of the steps make you feel excited and driven?

Does any of the steps make you feel unsure and anxious?

Write down which steps created a negative emotion for you.

Think about what decisions you have made in the past that may be contributing to this uneasy emotion, and decide what needs to be unlearned for you to move forward rather than away from your ideal Unique Signature.

If we feel anxious about narrowing our options, it normally indicates we have been off track in the past. If we choose to reflect on our feelings of anxiety, we can use these emotions positively to establish our true heading. Remember, these innate feelings are an accurate tool in guiding us towards the right path.

Correcting Your Course

Once we have *observed* the opportunity, *gathered the information* needed to complete our due diligence and *narrowed our options* to make it happen, we are on our way towards successfully creating our ideal Unique Signature. However, life doesn't always run so smoothly. The universe has a habit of presenting some difficulties or other opportunities just when we think we have it all under control. When this occurs, it is worth reflecting on our chosen pathway and making any corrections needed to stay on course.

Think about travelling from one destination to another in a car. Along the way we can sometimes experience unforeseen road closures that can alter our familiar route. When this happens, we don't turn around, go home and give up; we find a different route to ensure we arrive at the planned destination. Life should be no different from this analogy. When we have set our pathway towards achieving what we want to do and who we want to be, correcting our course, when needed, should be as easy as travelling down a different road towards our desired destination.

In Week 6, we discussed 'changing attitudes' and 'shifting our thinking' to successfully create our ideal Unique Signature. If we use these mindset strategies when narrowing our options and correcting our course, we are able to clearly see what needs to be altered and maintain our integrity in becoming our Unique Signature.

Weekly Task

List the different pathways that enable you to succeed in the opportunity you chose last week.

For each pathway, determine:

If there are any limiting beliefs you need to unlearn.

Any new strengths or abilities you will need to accomplish first.

Your intentions for pursuing each particular pathway. Will it be safe or challenging?

Any obligations and responsibilities that need to be finalised before moving forward with this opportunity.

Over the next week, take time to complete each step for each pathway you identify. The more pathways you scrutinise, the better prepared you will be to choose your ideal pathway, which will give you the ongoing confidence and enthusiasm needed to be successful.

Week 16

Deciding or Wishing

Choosing our next opportunity, conducting due diligence, narrowing our options, and correcting our course are the initial steps needed for making informed and genuine decisions towards creating what we want. However, once again, our mindset plays a very big part in whether a decision becomes a reality or not.

If we have the unrealistic notion that after making the decision to accomplish an opportunity, we can then sit back and wait for it to happen by magic, we will find there is no situation in this world where nothing happens magically by itself. The only magic that happens is the magic people create for themselves through their own deliberate efforts. These people are the ones who are successful in making their future the way they want it to be, by adopting the mindset of being positive, open-minded and confident, which may look like 'being lucky' to people around them.

The fact is if we decide to do nothing and surrender our efforts, we are relinquishing authority over our life. Consequently, people will interject and begin to organise our life for us. If we continually allow others' decisions to interfere with our ideal Unique Signature, or we wait for this elusive magic to happen, we are actually *wishing* our lives away. This may create insecurity and false hope in our life and for our future. There is no personal gain in wishing for things to happen; we must make it happen ourselves.

> '**Your wish is my command, and all commands require deliberate effort.**'
> — S.T.

Making a decision without deliberate effort is a recipe for frustration, disappointment and regret. Focusing our efforts on an area of our life establishes what our future is to become. Everything we do now mirrors where we will be in our future. For example, if we wish to lose weight and get fit but spend all our time on the lounge watching television, this will reflect our future, still *wishing* to lose weight. If we decide to live our life with deliberate effort, we have fewer negative emotions and create a more positive and sustainable true self.

Individual Activity

Have a close look at all your aspirations on your vision board.

Identify which aspirations you are genuinely deciding to achieve and which ones you are only wishing to achieve.

Reorganise your vision board to reflect which genuine decisions are priorities for you at this stage in your life.

Not focusing on the aspirations we are *wishing* to happen at this stage in our life does not mean we abandon them altogether. In the future, our wishes may become genuine decisions and consequently, with deliberate effort, they may become reality. Remember, being honest with ourselves is vital in making the right decisions that match our intentions and values to become our ideal Unique Signature.

What Brings You Joy

Knowing ourselves is a constructive way to create the ideal situations that will bring us joy. With every decision made that maintains our feeling of joy, we are likely to be more determined to achieve the outcome and not give up halfway. Once we are aware of this feeling and embrace it, making decisions and creating the magic of success for ourselves gets easier. Reflecting on our wins can be a very good indication of what brings us joy, and can establish we are making the right choices to remain in alignment with our ideal Unique Signature.

Discussion

Referring to your Week 4 weekly task, what were the three wins you achieved that week?

Once you achieved these three wins, did you reward yourself?

Did achieving these three wins bring you joy?

When we were young, we had a natural gift for doing what brought us joy through the innocence of playing, make-believe, cuddling up with the family pet, and exploring our house and garden. As we get older, we sometimes forget the simple things in life that bring us joy. We become wrapped up in the everyday duties of our life. We may think ourselves a little too old to play make-believe, yet wishing for something is exactly the same. The difference is that when we were children, we were cared for by our parents or guardians and they made all decisions on our behalf. Nevertheless, we are now in the unique situation of having endless opportunities to turn our wishes/make-believe into realities of joy; we just need to believe that making our own genuine decisions and choosing to follow through with deliberate effort will lead to the magic and the joy we are striving towards.

When we identify what brings us joy, we produce a natural chain reaction of positive emotions, which are an expression of all that is of value to us. This powerfully contributes towards our health and wellbeing. It has been medically proven that laughter and joy can assist with the healing process in illness. The feelings of happiness, jubilation, laughter, pleasure, and contentment, to name a few, also confirm we are in alignment with our ideal Unique Signature.

'The human race has one really effective weapon, and that is laughter.'

— Mark Twain

Weekly Task

Look at the list you made last week of the different pathways for your chosen opportunity.

Establish which pathways are genuine decisions for what you want to achieve, and which are wishes you hope to achieve.

Take this week to choose which genuine pathway will be best suited to bringing you joy at this stage of your life.

When choosing the best pathway to bring joy, we might consult our vision board buddy, a close family member or a friend. Sharing our feelings of joy and celebrating our wins with other people is a positive way to develop our confidence and self-belief. However, be aware that the people who are closest to us may not want to give up the familiarity of the person they know. It's ok to agree to disagree. Also, when making the final decision about your chosen pathway, it's important to remain mindful about who we are striving to be.

Week 17

Setting a Goal

Any success in our life is not built on something out of nothing. Our life is built on what we invest in it. If we invest enthusiasm, effort and persistence in our goal, then we will achieve it. On the contrary, if we do nothing to achieve what we want, we will achieve exactly that: nothing.

It is very common for people to prefer a less demanding lifestyle, choose the easy path or just go with the flow. The fact is, choosing the simplest path without a plan or strategy for our future may not result in the less demanding lifestyle we originally expected. When we choose the 'easy way', we approach things with less drive and enthusiasm, as we expect that something easy requires less effort. Yet we may then find ourselves in a situation where we are not naturally being ourselves, which can be draining and leave us feeling exhausted and lethargic in our immediate lifestyle choices. For example, if we choose to spend our days watching TV and not contributing to society, we are obviously taking an easy approach to life. However, this decision brings with it many limiting factors, such as dull life experiences, lack of money and diminishing living standards that can result in stress and poor health and affect our overall wellbeing. Furthermore, if this is not in alignment with our Unique Signature, the easy way can result in heartbreak and feelings of frustration and disappointment towards our life, now and in the future.

> **'Our negative emotions tell us we are out of alignment with our Unique Signature.'**
> — S.T.

Discussion

Can you identify any pathways you have taken just because they looked like the 'easy way'?

Did you discover that these easy pathways didn't create the simpler lifestyle you were seeking at the time?

There are typically two types of conversations a person can have: a purposeful conversation and a social conversation. Although social conversations are required for our natural interactions with people, many of us get wrapped up in the dramas of other people's lives, our lives or the lives of those we see on social media. Constantly having social conversations that last for hours, where each participant walks away without achieving anything but wasted time, places our ideal Unique Signature of less importance compared to the insignificant dramas we entertained. It is in our nature to focus on what's important to us, and so how we spend our leisure time reflects this. When we are focused on our ideal Unique Signature, we begin having purposeful conversations and we complete activities that benefit us in adopting the behaviours and habits we need to succeed.

Purposeful conversations are where the magic in our life is created. Once we are focused on a particular goal, purposeful conversations with like-minded people begin to happen. They help us to open our mind and become aware of unseen opportunities that will contribute towards our future Unique Signature. Without setting ourselves a goal and having a plan to accomplish this goal, we can flounder for hours, days, weeks, months, and even years and not accomplish our ideal success in life.

Individual Activity

What do your conversations with people sound like?

Is your focus mainly on the negative dramas around you and them?

How often do you discuss personal aspirations and positive outcomes with people?

Do you discuss matters of interest with people who are creating their own magic?

When we commit to achieving what we say we are going to do, we have fewer thoughts and discussions about the things that are not in alignment with our goal. When we have a plan and the strategies needed to complete our goals, we focus on the positive aspects that direct our energy towards achieving what we want in life, eliminating all the things we don't want. This reduces the 'numbness towards life' we can experience from time to time through meaningless, time-wasting interactions.

Setting a goal and using effective strategies is a straightforward and productive solution to the easy pathway we all want in our life. Also, by setting small goals we have a better chance of achieving the greater objective of reaching our chosen goal. With our knowledge of *decision-making strategies* (observation, gathering information, narrowing our options, and correcting our course), we can create the simpler lifestyle and the magic we deserve.

As covered in the previous chapter, there are many pathways we can take to achieving any opportunity after deciding on the goal that will bring us most joy. We then need to decide on an appropriate time frame to achieve our goals. Ideally, goals should be planned over a year. If we set our yearly goal and work towards our chosen pathway, we create plausible and successful circumstances. If we set our goals too high, there is a chance that we will lose interest and the stamina to keep going.

With each goal set there is also a need to complete our due diligence by observing every opportunity that will assist us; gather the information needed to make informed decisions; narrow our options to obtain the best results; and correct our course where required to establish the success for what we want and who we want to be.

Weekly Task

Look at the list you made last week of your genuine decisions/ pathways to achieve success in your chosen opportunity.

List all the small goals you need to accomplish your chosen pathway.

Over the next week, prioritise these small goals for completion.

Reflect on the following:

Are your strengths and knowledge adequate for each goal?

If not, what additional strengths and knowledge do you need first?

Record how you feel about approaching each goal. Let your internal guidance system help you to decide your next step.

The task of using *decision-making strategies* may seem tedious to some, and the urge to 'just jump in' and make it happen may be overpowering. However, it is very important to reflect on what has and has not worked in the past. The more vigilant we are with this process, the smoother things will fall into place in the future. The more often we practise these strategies, the more they become habit, and habits shape our character and destiny.

Week 18

Your Responsibility to You

Congratulations, we are now two-thirds along our pathway towards Knowing Our Own Success. We now need to reflect on everything that has been presented so far. Over the past 17 weeks, we have explored what is needed to succeed in the lifestyle we want and what is required for us to be the person we want to be. Completing each activity has given us the necessary scaffolding to make our ideal Unique Signature a reality. By first understanding our weaknesses, strengths and abilities, recognising what and who is holding us back, and knowing what limiting beliefs need to be unlearned, we are able to overcome challenges and adopt the correct mindset to move towards our true potential. By always being conscious of our intentions, values and posture, we initiate within ourselves the strength and wisdom required to engage and succeed in our ideal future.

Recognising these attributes, while building a constructive way of thinking, is only one aspect towards achieving our big picture in life. Everyone knows the old saying 'practice makes perfect'. To accomplish the lifestyle we want, practice is vital for our success. If we fall back into old habits, we may alter what we have recently accomplished and move away from our ideal Unique Signature. It is our responsibility to ensure this does not happen.

Discussion

Have you returned to any old habits?

Are these old habits hindering your ideal Unique Signature?

What course corrections do you need to make to move forward?

By establishing habits that support our ideal future, we achieve a sense of accomplishment and pride. It is in our best interest to remain true to our chosen pathway and values to create the drive and dedication needed to move towards our ultimate goal.

The weekly activities so far presented have given us time, without pressure, to adopt any new behaviours and habits to occur naturally. We may sometimes become disconnected from our overall goal, but it is our responsibility to stay focused on the big picture: what we want from life and who we want to be. If we neglect all we have worked towards over the past 17 weeks, we will be abandoning what we need in order to experience our own rewards, continuing instead only to reap the rewards of what others bestow on us.

Individual Activity

How many weekly activities have you genuinely completed over the past 17 weeks?

List the activities you attempted half-heartedly and state why you chose not to complete each activity. For example:

Was it because of someone's opinion?

Was it lack of time?

Did you feel it was not important?

Was it because of fear?

Did it seem too difficult to complete at the time?

Or was your comfort zone too familiar and convenient?

Giving your honest reflection on each statement reinforces that you are being truthful to your Unique Signature.

> **'Great accomplishments in life are always achieved outside our comfort zone.'**
>
> — S.T.

The comfort zone is not a mystical place where unexplained phenomena occur. It is a dull and lifeless plane, where most of us spend large amounts of time in a state of existence, instead of living. Living is defined as 'being active and thriving; having a livelihood to experience and enjoy to the fullest'. On the other hand, existence is defined as a 'state of being' and nothing more. By continuing to take refuge in our comfort zone, we focus on our vulnerabilities and create insecurities within our life. To live our lives entirely within the comfort zone is neither healthy nor beneficial and it undermines our ability to thrive and experience our life to the fullest.

By stepping out of our comfort zone, we take responsibility for our Unique Signature and the lifestyle we want.

Completing each weekly activity enhances our ability to do so, confidently. Having the discipline to embrace what we are capable of in our life is refusing to relinquish authority over our life to someone else: close friends, family members, partners/spouse, or even general social dependence. Other people may believe they have our best interest at heart, but their intervention interferes with the development of our Unique Signature.

Weekly Task

Over this week, revisit each weekly activity and establish, from your notes, what portion of your ideal Unique Signature is being neglected.

Make a stand this week and decide to embrace every activity to achieve your fullest potential!

Remember. This is your life, to live it the way you feel fit to live it. Be honest, stand tall and continue moving towards what will strengthen your experiences in life. Enjoy them to the fullest.

> **'It had long since come to my attention that People of accomplishment rarely sat back and let things happen to them. They went out and happened to things.'**
> **— Leonardo DaVinci**

Part Three: Know Your Own Success

'Know Your Own Success' is the next part of our journey in accomplishing our ideal Unique Signature. From this stage onwards, we will explore the actions needed while continually developing our mindset towards establishing our intentions and values.

What if we could change our life by changing how we react towards different situations? Every life event we experience, positive or negative, reflects on how we react to different circumstances. If our reactions are not in alignment with our ideal Unique Signature, we may sometimes create undesirable outcomes. What if we could experience better results every day by adopting a different response to the circumstances in our lives?

By implementing proven strategies that will develop our life objectives, we will enhance our circumstances, wellbeing and self-confidence, which will influence our ideal Unique Signature and our destiny in life.

The 'Knowing Yourself' and 'Knowing Your Intention' activities are closely connected to the 'Know Your Own Success' activities. Every action we take reflects directly on the decisions we make and the mindset we adopt when choosing the best pathway. The actions we take also deeply reflect on who we are and who we want to be, which have a huge impact on all stages of our life.

Week 19

Act or be Acted Upon

Have you ever wanted to do something that you were excited about but decided not to do because of peer pressure? We have all experienced feelings of regret and frustration around this type of experience. This experience describes 'being acted upon'. Being acted upon is when someone else dictates what we should or shouldn't do. They don't necessarily say the words 'don't do that', but we feel manipulated by what they do and say, such as their body language and posture indicating their disapproval, or even comments like, 'what do you want to do that for?', or 'that's stupid'. Peer pressure also occurs when someone influences us to do something we don't want to do, such as participating in a prank or dangerous activity.

Discussion

Can you think of a time when you didn't do what you wanted due to peer pressure?

How did this make you feel?

The influence of people can also occur when we are deciding on our next step towards our desired lifestyle. When people observe others in the midst of an exciting change, they naturally want to be involved and not get left behind. This display of support can be used to our advantage; however, it is important we *act* according to our desire, to ensure we are following our direction, not theirs. Although people may think they have our best interests at heart, if it is not in alignment with our Unique Signature then we are being *acted upon*.

As previously explained, our actions are in direct correlation with our intentions, which reflect our thoughts. Most people think our thoughts occur mostly on autopilot and therefore we have no control over our actions and circumstances. To engage and act towards what we desire is recognising we do have control over our thoughts, intentions, circumstances, and actions to achieve any desired outcome we seek.

Our circumstances are defined as 'the existing conditions or state of affairs of our surroundings'. Choosing to act or not to act creates the experience of either positive or negative circumstances, which purely depend on whether we are accomplishing the things in life we want to accomplish. For example, if we had our sights set on getting our driver's licence but couldn't be bothered obtaining our learner's permit or attending driving lessons, we would be creating the circumstance of having to rely on others for transport. This example would be a negative circumstance because we are not achieving what we aspire to. By actively overcoming our weaknesses and creating new strengths and abilities, we build positive circumstances that create joy in our life.

Individual Activity

Think back to when You acted on a decision that created a negative circumstance.

Is this circumstance likely to be the same for the next two years?

Do you need to take any other actions to create the circumstances that will reflect your ideal Unique Signature?

It is very important to realise that our circumstances today are only a reflection of what we have created in the past and that they hold no truth or certainty for what will happen in our future. We all have the unique ability to change our circumstances if we don't like them. Changing any circumstance requires an inspired action. Whenever we have an inspired thought, we must act upon it. Don't delay, don't second guess and don't doubt when an opportunity presents itself and you have the impulse to act; just do it. Referring to your decision-making strategies will help with this process. Don't dwell on the negative aspects of what needs to be overcome when you have an inspiring thought. If you must dwell on something, dwell on the result to achieve your ideal Unique Signature. If you remain in the state of wishing and not acting, you will never experience the joy of knowing our own success.

Weekly Task

When was the last time you said to yourself, 'Let's just do it'?

List five tasks you have been meaning to do in the last couple of weeks but haven't.

Will any of these tasks change your current circumstances?

Refer to your vision board and determine if these tasks will assist you to be in alignment with your ideal Unique Signature.

During this week, genuinely choose to engage and act to complete each task with inspired and deliberate actions.

To act and not be acted upon is to take control of our circumstances, continuing to enhance our ability to open our mind to new and exciting opportunities and create the future we want.

> **'Our future is what we make it.'**
>
> — S.T.

Week 20

Procrastination

We are all creatures of habit, and procrastination is a common one. It is the biggest killer of our vision and it inhibits achievement of our ideal Unique Signature. Procrastination is a silent battle between our 'lazy self' and our 'driven self'. While our driven self is the advocate of our ideal Unique Signature, our lazy self will attempt many things in order not to undertake productive activities that are necessary for achieving our ideal future.

Examples are budgeting for self-education, a car, house, or dream holiday. Our driven self would research the cost of what we want, our total income and all regular bills, then create a budget for weekly savings to make it happen. Sounds simple enough; however, our lazy self on the way to researching the information would see the fridge and stop to inspect it even when we're not hungry, then stop to pat the dog, then see the phone and decide to call a friend, then... Sound familiar?

Discussion

Think about your most common lazy self impulses you have that put off productive activities.

Do your lazy self habits affect your everyday life?

Are your lazy self habits delaying your ideal Unique Signature?

When we were younger and learning things for the first time, we had the innate drive to *want* to achieve things today, not tomorrow. We *wanted* to write our own name without help; *wanted* to tie our own shoe laces; *wanted* to climb the highest monkey-bars; *wanted* to run and ride the fastest. We had a driven self that overruled our lazy self. Our young internal creativity and enthusiasm gave us the strength to succeed whatever we set our mind to and the confidence to communicate what we *wanted*. As we age, we adopt the unnatural habit of procrastinating, by not communicating our intentions or not acting with purpose to achieve what we desire.

By procrastinating, we establish the unnatural condition of being our biggest weakness, which in turn can contribute to an unhealthy absence of trust in our ability to succeed. This is accompanied by a lack of commitment towards our ideal future, a lack of accountability for our decisions and actions that reflect our ideal Unique Signature; and inattention towards achieving the results that align with what we want and who we want to be. These may all cause us to be acted upon, instead of taking action towards our success and experiencing the happiness from doing so.

'Procrastination is one of the most common and deadliest of diseases and its toll on success and happiness is heavy.'
— Wayne Gretzky

Being Assertive

Being assertive does not mean being aggressive, arrogant or unapproachable to the views, opinions or productive advice from other people. It means having the ability to communicate what we want for ourselves and deciding to act when an opportunity arises. Communicating our needs, wants and feelings to people directly and honestly respects our Unique Signature and others around us. Our assertive communications reflect the expression of our intentions and are the middle ground between being passive and aggressive.

A lack of persistence can also affect our driven self. Most of us are good starters but poor finishers. This often happens when we try something new and the result is different from what we originally planned; or when we apply for our dream job without success; or when we try to lose weight and stop dieting when we experience an off day. We give up at the first sign of adversity or defeat and allow our procrastinating lazy self to take over.

Procrastination is the passive behavioural trait of our lazy self, and so assertiveness is a sure way to change the dynamics and ensure our positive driven self engages in the pursuit of our success. If we consciously observe our lazy self and what it hinders, and what our driven self excels in, we can then reflect truthfully on what helps us remain in alignment with our ideal Unique Signature.

Individual Activity

Give an example of what your driven self looks like for the following attributes:

Trusting in your ability.

Being committed to your ideal future.

Being accountable for your decisions and actions.

Paying attention to results that indicate you are in alignment with your ideal Unique Signature.

Our driven self will prevail over our habits of procrastination every time when we:

- Remain assertive and create a realistic time frame for our yearly successes.
- Trust our strengths and our ability to overcome weaknesses.
- Persist in our commitment to creating our ideal future.
- Are accountable for our decisions and actions.
- Pay attention to the results that are in alignment with our ideal Unique Signature.

Weekly Task

Refer to the pathway you genuinely decided to accomplish from Week 16 and create a checklist for the following:

What time frame have you set aside to achieve this pathway?

What productive activities have you undertaken so far to make this pathway a reality?

What abilities do you trust within yourself to make this happen?

What habits have you displayed towards being committed to accomplishing this pathway?

What decisions and actions are you being accountable for towards achieving this?

What results are you paying attention to as evidence of being in alignment with your ideal pathway?

Are you being persistent so that you remain focused on your goals to accomplish this pathway?

There is no substitute for assertiveness. By making assertiveness our motto, we will discover that procrastination disappears from our thoughts, intentions and habits. Procrastination cannot exist when assertiveness prevails.

Week 21

Feeling Out of Control

Our emotions are a very important aspect for how we experience our life circumstances and how we act upon them. When we are feeling out of control, we perceive our life as very gloomy and risk becoming a victim of our circumstances. We may blame others and the world around us for everything that does not seem ideal in our life.

A person may achieve a high education, obtain a top-earning job and live in an expensive house in an exotic location. However, if this person continually experiences negative emotions and feels out of control, perceiving their life as not ideal and bleak, they will become stressed and frustrated with their circumstances, leading to disappointment, regret and depression, no matter how perfect their life may seem to other people.

Everyone experiences negative emotions differently. Some people simply shrug them off and carry on, while some fall into the trap of allowing negative emotions to overpower them and consume their life. As our feelings influence our thoughts and vice-versa, being out of control adversely affects how we act and what we think about our circumstances, our self, people, and our surroundings.

Discussion

Reflect on a time when you have felt your emotions were out of control.

How did your circumstances feel to you?

Did you allow these negative feelings to overpower your life?

When we feel out of control, we tend to constantly think negative thoughts. We only recall the bad things that have happened in our life and shunt the good thoughts deep inside. For example, a group of friends going out to a concert will later recall the funny conversations of the night, the excitement of the live entertainment, the delicious meal, and the good company. If one member of the same group was feeling out of control, they would recall the trip to the concert as uncomfortable and expensive, the seats too hard, the stage hard to see because of the person sitting in front of them, and the meal not cooked properly. There is no denying events of this nature can happen. However, these little things should not diminish our good thoughts.

Thinking positive or negative thoughts about our life is a reflection of our current mindset, which influences our emotional behaviours and how we experience our circumstances. Generally, people who think bad or negative thoughts see the glass as half empty and see one tree at a time (recurring problems). They have negative emotions that cause them to be out of control, they blame others for their circumstances and take no responsibility for their intentions and actions. People who think good or positive thoughts see the glass as half full and see the entire forest (problem solving). Their positive emotions control their life and they take responsibility for their intentions and actions.

It is important to identify what mindset we lean towards; whether we have good or bad memories, or positive or negative thoughts about our environment. Knowing this enables us to take control of our emotions and move forward in a healthy manner. This does not mean we will never experience negative emotions. On the contrary, in our lifetime we must experience the full range of emotions in order to adapt to new and challenging situations. Displaying a range of emotions lets people know what we are feeling and what our intentions are at a particular time, which is evident in our conversations and our physical posture. This awareness also gives us the gift of determining if we are in alignment with our ideal Unique Signature.

Individual Activity

Consider what you have experienced this week.

List all the positive and negative things that have happened to you this week.

Total them up. Are there more or fewer negative things than last week?

Are you adopting the correct mindset to succeed what you want for your future?

Our feelings and emotions indicate whether we are in alignment with our desires. The main reason we experience out-of-control emotions is because of a lack of self-discipline, which is needed for the correct mindset in order to remain in alignment with our desires.

> 'You may not control all the events that happen to you, but you can decide not to be reduced by them..'
> — Maya Angelou

Feeling in Control

Feeling in control is about self-discipline, which comes from exercising self-control over our emotions. This means controlling all negative thoughts and actions. Having self-control does not mean becoming desensitised and not able to express ourselves during diverse experiences. Self-control is about knowing when to display the appropriate emotion that will create the ideal circumstance we are seeking at the time.

If someone feels very hostile towards us, we may choose to react in one of two ways. We may raise our defences, demonstrate aggression back to the person and elevate the feelings of frustration and anger. Alternatively, we may demonstrate calmness, which will defuse the hostile situation and create a more manageable situation where tolerance and understanding can take place.

Generally, we exhibit frustration and anger because of our current situation rather than because of the other person.

Understanding this and not taking another's frustration and anger personally can help us manage our emotions during any unsettling situation.

Before we can control any challenging situation, we must first be able to control ourselves. Self-mastery of our emotions is the hardest job we will ever tackle. If we do not achieve self-control, we will surely be conquered by our self and by others. We may then constantly feel out of control and experience low self-esteem and a lack of confidence when attempting new and potentially exciting experiences.

To what extent we control our emotions is known as 'emotional intelligence'. Our emotional intelligence is very much aligned with our strengths and weaknesses, which change with the different stages we experience during our lifetime. As young children, our emotional intelligence is immature; we have a lot to learn about the world around us. We tend to cry or have a temper tantrum to get what we want without thinking of the consequences. As we mature, through the experiences of our diverse interactions with people, we become more self-aware and have a greater understanding of the consequences of our emotional actions and how they create our circumstances.

Emotional intelligence is knowing when and how to respond to a particular situation. Our engagement or avoidance behaviour reflects what we believe is worth fighting for or walking away from. Demonstrating self-discipline and self-control is about being responsible for our intentions, decisions, actions, and habits. It is also about not letting others act upon us, not blaming others for our lack of assertiveness and remaining persistent by staying focused on the ultimate prize – our ideal Unique Signature.

Weekly Task

What progress have you made with your chosen pathway?

Have you experienced any adversities that have made you angry or frustrated?

How did you handle your emotions in each situation? Were you aware of your emotions at the time?

Did you blame someone else for your lack of progress, or did you take control of your pathway?

Could you have managed your emotions differently to achieve a better result?

Over the next week, list how you could revisit each situation, demonstrating your emotional intelligence by having an appropriate emotion that will achieve a better result than before.

When we are in control of our emotions, we naturally adopt the positive mindset needed to open our mind to observe ideal opportunities, create meaningful interactions with people and accomplish the results and circumstances we want in life.

Week 22

Overcoming Fear

Fear is natural. Without it, we would not be able to distinguish between what is or is not important to us while progressing through the different stages of our life. Fear comes in different forms and our reactions depend on what makes us fearful. When we are in danger, fear is a natural defence mechanism enabling us to protect ourselves. For example, when we are crossing a busy road and hear a car horn, we react and get out of the way. Fear also alerts us to situations that are not healthy for our wellbeing, such as someone violating our personal safety. In this instant, it is very important we acknowledge this feeling and seek assistance from someone we trust.

Uncertainty is another type of fear that we experience when presented with something new or challenging. It is natural to second-guess ourselves, as we need to know we have 'ticked all the boxes' in order to be successful. This type of fear acknowledges our internal guidance system when embarking on something that is very important to us, such as attaining our driver's licence, attending a job interview, asking someone out, or speaking in public.

> 'I learned that courage was not the absence of fear, but the triumph over it.'
> — Nelson Mandela

Discussion

Reflect on when you achieved something that really mattered to you.

Consider what it was that made you determined to see it through, and embrace that feeling now.

Other fears we may experience is a result of not managing our basic natural fears of feeling nervous or in danger, which can develop into greater, unnatural fears. Post-traumatic stress, anxiety and phobias are unnatural fears that occur when people allow their basic fears to become out of control and consume them.

By letting our fears consume us, we are in jeopardy of delaying new and exciting experiences, which creates the circumstance of never accomplishing our dreams while remaining frozen in our ability and limiting our willingness to try anything. This leads to a smaller life and sometimes a separation from our true self and our loved ones.

Individual Activity

When was the last time you attempted something new or challenging?

Were you nervous about trying this experience?

Did you let your fears consume you and choose not to proceed? Or did you overcome your fears and enjoy the excitement of this new experience?

By choosing to overcome our fears and take control of our circumstances and our state of mind, we will manage these feelings of fear and work with our internal guidance system, enhancing our awareness of what we need to do to create our success.

Strategies

The following strategies for managing fears and developing our internal guidance system may be embraced individually or collectively. Some of our deeper fears may require us to adopt a more direct and deliberate effort to overcome them, and the following may help us to do so.

Strategy 1

What Brings Us Joy? Reflecting on what brings us joy, and thus generating positive emotions needed to outweigh negative emotions, gives us the strength to overcome fear. Some people are scared of snakes, so going to a reptile park would not bring them joy. If we do what brings us joy, what we fear will be shunted into the background and have no effect on our lifestyle or on our ideal Unique Signature. However, if a fear is stopping us from achieving what we want to do and who we want to be, it is extremely important to overcome it to ensure we experience the joy we deserve.

Strategy 2

Drawing on Our Strengths is the most important strategy needed to overcome our fears. Our strengths are our positive thoughts and affirmations and are ten times more powerful than our negative thoughts (Dr Denis Waitley). When we feel defeated by a fear, conquering this irrational feeling with strength affirms our authority over our life and mindset. For instance, if we fear change of the unknown, by reminiscing about a time when an outcome of an action we took resulted in an improved opportunity and circumstance, the feelings of joy, positivity and strength we felt then can be drawn on to overcome the next obstacle.

Strategy 3

Learning to Relax. When we feel defeated by a fear, our mind is clouded by negative thoughts. This creates a barrier, inhibiting our ability to focus on our strengths. By retreating to a location where we are at our most contented, and using relaxation techniques to suit our individual needs, we create the necessary ambience to focus on our strengths. Relaxation techniques do not only mean meditation. For some, it may be taking the dog for a walk, going for a run, boxing or martial arts, reading a book, listening to music, playing a musical instrument, or playing a computer game. You choose, it's *your* happy place.

Strategy 4

Adopting a New Posture to relax body, mind and spirit. Once we conquer a fear and feel in control, our posture is calm and confident. During our relaxation techniques, we can relax by unclenching our jaw, softening our forehead, opening our fists, and breathing slowly to ease our pounding heart. Taking mini-breaks throughout the day and learning to live in the relaxed state we deserve will prove very healthy for our wellbeing.

Strategy 5

Shifting Our Thinking on how we react to fear is the difference between taking control of or being consumed by fear. If our reaction is to avoid doing something new or challenging because we fear a failed outcome, a shift in our thinking can help overcome this mindset. Building structure into our daily schedule can create a feeling of safety and the strength needed to battle through any fear that threatens to consume us. An example is to set aside an hour each day to explore and research the possibility of doing something we have always wanted to do, and then resuming our normal daily routine. When this one hour a day of structured curiosity becomes a habit in our daily routine, we become more familiar and comfortable with the idea of physically accomplishing the event. This will then require no greater effort, as our mind will already have accepted it and we will have overcome the fear that once consumed us.

Strategy 6

Knowing Our Intention and Our Habits can help us control our fears. Our fears are simply illusions that we sometimes exaggerate, making up frightening stories about our past and our future, while rehearsing them in our mind until we are terrified. Our stories about fear are often related to pain experienced in the past, or the fear of being hurt in the future. We can change the fearful stories we tell ourselves by creating habits that make us feel safe. We can live in the present moment and create new stories filled with positive intentions about our future expectations.

Strategy 7

Setting a Goal to overcome our fear. If we are faced with an irrational fear that is detrimental to our ideal lifestyle, facing it head-on is the best antidote. By setting a goal, making a list about how we intend overcoming the fear and stating a time frame, we are making a deliberate effort to overcome the fear. If the fear has been very debilitating, it is important to start with small, realistic goals to achieve small wins in overcoming the fear. For example, if we fear speaking in public, we might join a small group of speakers (school debate or toastmasters) and begin facing our fear by introducing ourselves to the group. We might then decide to give a speech within two months of joining.

Strategy 8

Deciding, Not Wishing and Having Faith in our ability to accomplish anything we set our mind to. After setting a goal, we must be assertive in overcoming our fear, not just wish it away. When we adopt a driven mindset and establish habits of determined action, all we need to do is have faith in our ability to make it happen.

Strategy 9

Counting Our Wins when we make progress in controlling our fears. We tend to beat ourselves up when we fail and fail to celebrate when we succeed. No matter how small the progress is, we need to count the win and celebrate it with a close family member, friend or vision board buddy. This enhances the power of our positive intention. Negativity cannot exist in the presence of our healthy positive mindset.

Strategy 10

Course Correcting to ensure we are on track to eliminating our irrational fear. Overcoming a fear that has disillusioned us for a while can be daunting and may take time to accomplish. Along the way, course corrections may be needed to remain assertive, driven and confident. We need to take small steps, keep the big picture in sight and have faith in our success.

If we delay in establishing healthy habits, we continue to allow our fears to consume and dominate us.

> 'Face your fears and doubts,
> and new worlds will open to you.'
> — Robert Kiyosaki

Weekly Task

During this week, practise managing your fears by becoming familiar with the strategy or strategies that suit you best.

Identify a fear you want to overcome. Start with a fear that is not too overwhelming:

1. Think about what brings you joy and consider if this fear is stopping you from experiencing the joy you want.
2. Reminisce about a time when you experienced a positive result and draw on this strength to conquer your fear.
3. Find or return to a place and/or activity where you feel relaxed and contented. Let your mind drift towards thoughts of conquering this fear.
4. While in your 'happy place', adopt a relaxing posture as described and embrace the healthy feeling of conquering this fear.
5. Research and plan to achieve one thing your fear is preventing you from attempting and mastering (Week 14 can help here).
6. When you hear your mind telling you an exaggerated horror story, rewrite the ending so that it is instead filled with positive intentions. Acknowledge the present moment for what it actually is.

7. Set yourself a realistic goal and a time frame for conquering this fear.
8. When experiencing the fear, decide with determination to react to the fear differently from the way you would normally (engage not avoid, calmness not anger).
9. Count your wins, no matter how small.
10. At the end of this week, reflect on how you have progressed towards conquering this fear and make any course corrections needed.

From this point onwards, regularly revisiting these ten strategies will help us feel confident about conquering our fears.

Week 23

Temporary Setbacks

Many of us find ourselves in undesirable circumstances due to not knowing how to triumph over the temporary setbacks we experience in everyday life. If allowed, these everyday setbacks can hinder our lifestyle and ideal Unique Signature from becoming a reality. Many of the setbacks we experience are simply weaknesses waiting to be transformed into strengths. All setbacks are therefore only temporary and can easily be remedied.

Lack of Knowledge

This can easily be resolved by self-education (Week 1). Indecisions and lack of a definite plan to gain the knowledge needed to create better circumstances for our lifestyle can result in ongoing undesired circumstances. Self-education can make us a fortune, not only in financial terms but in living the life we aspire to.

Lack of Wisdom

We may have the knowledge but we may not know how to use it. Completing decision-making strategies (Week 14) can develop the wisdom we need to move forward with deliberate action.

Lack of Vision

This is one of the most destructive setbacks. If we struggle with knowing what we want and who we want to be (Week 2), this setback will linger until we choose our ideal future and act upon it. Establishing what brings us joy can assist with knowing our intention and our vision for the future.

Lack of Enthusiasm

Our enthusiasm comes from within and reflects our desires. It is imperative to strive towards what is important to us and to be aware of our wants and values (Week 11) to generate the drive we need to succeed.

Lack of Self-Discipline

This may result in unwanted consequences and circumstances. If we demonstrate reckless and impulsive behaviours without using our emotional intelligence (Week 21), such as acting before thinking and analysing a situation, our intentions become volatile and may lead to insecure situations for us and the people we interact with.

Lack of Assertive Decisions

If we lack assertiveness, continually changing our mind about a decision made or making half-hearted decisions (Weeks 12 and 20), we are not truly committed to achieving a planned outcome. This leads to ongoing unnecessary setbacks and constant course corrections.

Lack of Effort

This happens when we want something to happen but don't make any effort to make it happen (Weeks 16 and 20). A lack of effort can also create a 'lazy self' lifestyle and result in poor wellbeing. This setback can be reversed by adopting our driven self and acting upon what we truly want.

Lack of Tolerance

This can easily be remedied by being empathetic. Most of us are frustrated at times by the actions of people, which may cause feelings of negativity towards another's success or failure. Adopting the correct attitude and posture (Weeks 6 and 9) can develop our emotional intelligence and also assist with overcoming other setbacks.

Lack of Funds

This may be a convenient excuse not to do something. If we perform our due diligence (Week 14), we can wisely establish the funds needed to absorb any temporary financial setback. By planning small achievable goals, we can find a solution to any financial problem. If we truly want it to happen, we will find the money to make it happen.

Lack of Persistence

This may be the result of any combination of the above setbacks. Many of us give up after only one failure, or hear about someone who falls in defeat, never to rise again, allowing temporary setbacks to devour their drive. What about the people who engage in their life? The ones who gain knowledge from their unfortunate experiences and succumb to the irresistible power of persistence to rise again? Often, it is only after the success reveals itself that we recognise the major part that persistence played.

Discussion

Reflect on an achievement because you refused to give up.

Consider what you would have lost if you had not persisted.

Persistence is the backbone of success. Persistence is our ability to stay focused and maintain our course of action regardless of how we are feeling. If we feel like quitting because of the many setbacks we encounter, persistence will conquer them and construct our ideal circumstances. By simply taking action, we will eventually get the results we are seeking, and this will provide the motivation to continue our future successes.

> **'Success is the result of persistence and learning from failures.'**
> **— Unknown**

Troubleshooting

Every failure brings with it a seed of knowledge containing the equivalent advantage to that of the failure. The advantage is in learning from our mistakes and gaining strength and knowledge. Without failure we would not progress and society would not be inspired to invent new products or make advances in medicine and science.

Many great inventions have been discovered by learning from a failure. Charles Goodyear, attempting to invent a new durable tyre, mixed rubber with sulphur. He failed miserably in creating a new advanced tyre but invented plastic instead. Without such new knowledge arising from failures, society would not have progressed and many technologies would not exist today.

Individual Activity

Spend some time researching other inventions that have been discovered due to an epic fail.

Have you discovered new and wonderful experiences from a personal failure?

Much of what we discover from our failures contributes to our problem-solving and troubleshooting abilities. 'If I do this instead, this will happen and I will get what I want.' The human race is very good at improvising and adapting to overcome adversity. Most of us do this in the kitchen: if we are making a sandwich and we do not have butter, we may use mayo or sauce instead; we may make a coffee with cream if we have run out of milk. We take such simple things for granted but we need to acknowledge them for what they represent: our initiative to obtain what we want. We also need to acknowledge the versatility of our natural ability to problem-solve. If we are able to apply this troubleshooting ability to simple tasks, it is then logical to assume we can apply the same ability to more complex tasks.

Troubleshooting skills can be broken down into three main factors – how, what and why. Understanding *how* something works is the first step to troubleshooting any problem. We are then able to ascertain *what* is needed to be replaced or *what* actions must be taken. The final factor is *why* we believe something will work.

If we analyse these factors while troubleshooting any problem, the most effective skill we use is simply *making a genuine decision*. When troubleshooting any problem, make the decision promptly and change your mind slowly. If you don't succeed the first time, don't change your mind due to this one failure. Re-evaluate how, what and why it didn't work, then course correct where required.

Weekly Task

Consider any setback you have experienced.

For each setback:

Note how this setback came about.

Note what is required to be done to overcome this setback.

Note why you believe this solution will work.

Note why overcoming this setback will contribute to your Unique Signature.

Identify and list the newfound wisdom and abilities created by these setbacks.

Week 24

Action with Purpose

In life, we sometimes move forward and at other times, we stand still or go backwards when seeking to achieve our goals. Our objective in life should always be to go forward with deliberate action. Action with purpose is about having a practical plan of action we can comfortably use to fulfil our desired outcomes. In Weeks 12 and 13, we discussed the different decisions people instinctively make, such as one person making a quick decision whereas another considers every detail before making a decision. Our unique plan of action reflects our decision-making strategies. The action taken may be ideal for one person but not necessarily ideal for another. Whatever the action, it is important to be consistent and move forward in a positive manner.

Discussion

Reflect on a time when you wanted something (an object or an experience).

Did you have a practical plan to act with purpose to make it a reality?

If yes, did you find that everything fell nicely into place, with minimum fuss to achieve what you wanted?

If no, could you have formulated a plan to act with purpose to achieve what you wanted?

When our thoughts are backed by strong desire, they tend to transform into physical actions with purpose. When we have a desire, it is our responsibility to act upon it. However, if we do not have a plan of action our efforts can waver and we may go around in circles or have to repeat many times what we have already attempted, with minimum results.

Let's relate this to joining a gym to get fit. If we make little effort and attend the gym only now and then, we do not get any fitter and we waste our resources (money), thus going around in circles by complaining about not getting fit, even with a gym membership. If we had a plan of action to attend the gym consistently, our results would support our efforts. We all have the opportunity to partake in the freedom of any opportunity we want, but only when we participate in what we want with effort is this freedom apparent.

Our purpose in life is simply what we say it is and how we act to achieve it. Occasional efforts towards accomplishing what we want have no value to our Unique Signature. People who talk about what they are 'going to do' too much and demonstrate little to no effort towards any action, give the impression of having great knowledge about life achievements, while not experiencing any. They talk too much and do little else, only occasionally working towards their ideal goals. If we talk more than we listen and are acted upon more than we take action, we are depriving ourselves of many opportunities for accumulating useful knowledge and wisdom which would help us with any life experience we desire.

We must be vigilant about what we want to achieve, as we are more motivated and effective when we are striving towards our Unique Signature. Self-analysis of how we feel about our life experiences will tell us if we have advanced, what advancements we have made and how effectively or slowly. Our internal guidance system will also tell us if we have taken any backward steps because of feelings of regret and disappointment. If we feel driven and excited, we are on the correct path towards acting with purpose. Revising our decision-making strategies when in doubt helps us determine what to do next.

> 'Listen to what your internal guidance system is telling you.'
>
> — S.T.

Action with Passion

Once we have a practical plan of deliberate action, we need to ask ourselves, 'Does this resonate with my heart?' Nothing can be acquired without being open to receiving it (Rhonda Byrne). If we pay attention to what we are attracted to, we instinctively adopt an attitude of openness and allowance to receive this into our life.

Many people will never be wealthy or successful because they believe they don't deserve it. The truth is, whatever we are passionate about is what we deserve. Many people have a false belief that there is not enough in the world to go around. The good news is that everyone in the world does not want the same success, and everyone's idea of success is unique. Many of us have the instilled belief that 'we must get a good education to get a good job' and 'only rich people are successful'. Success is much more than our job or how much money we have in the bank. Success is about taking up an idea with passion and making that idea our Unique Signature for the life we desire. If we let our brain, muscles, nerves – every part of our body – be consumed by the idea of our success, we allow ourselves to act with passion, without fear, and receive the results we are entitled to, reaping the rewards that reflect our efforts.

Individual Activity

You may use your Vision Board to assist you with this activity.

Think about what you are passionate about (world peace, your education, your job, your home, your creativity, your knowledge, your pets, your sport).

Has any of your life experiences and actions been driven by your passion?

Do you believe you could be successful in any of these areas of your life?

Can you see there is enough of this type of success to go around?

Coordinated action and commitment towards what we are passionate about help us move forward to success. The following checklist can be used to ensure we are striving towards our passion with deliberate actions.

Checking our Intention

Do our intentions fulfil our passion in life and our Unique Signature?

Set the Scene

Have we adopted the correct mindset and attitude to enable us to move forward with our purposeful actions?

Check Prior Commitments

Do our current actions clash with any prior commitments? Do we need to complete something before we start something new?

Check Setbacks

Have we attempted this type of action before? If so, what needs to change for our success to become a reality this time? Refer to last week's activity.

Check Perspective

Can we see the big picture? Can we visualise our success in achieving our goal?

Check Feelings and Impact

Does this action with purpose meet our passion? Are we doing this for our own desire or for someone else's?

Make a Commitment

We must say, 'Yes, I commit' or 'No, I don't commit'. There is no in-between. Our 'yes' means nothing if we are unable to say 'no' or 'decide to act' or 'not to act'. It is our decision and we must be passionate about it to experience success.

Weekly Task

Using the checklist above, write a plan of action for building success from what you are passionate about.

Use other skills you have gained while completing the weekly course of activities.

Allocate some time during each week to develop this passion into the success you deserve it to be.

Week 25

Taking Responsibility

Taking responsibility for our actions is acknowledging our failures, our setbacks, our accomplishments, and our circumstances. So far in Part Three, we have explored several factors that affect our ability to manage our attitude, actions, and behaviours. If we procrastinate, are out of control, are acted upon, are consumed by our fears, or do not troubleshoot our setbacks, we are relinquishing our responsibility and developing undesired circumstances. On the contrary, if we are assertive, take action when required, act passionately, overcome our fears, and troubleshoot any setback that may arise, we are then taking responsibility to develop the desired circumstances for our success.

To take responsibility for our actions we need to be driven and have willpower. It is an easy escape to make excuses and not take responsibility. However, this will eventually make it increasingly difficult to achieve anything we want. People with little willpower can be easily persuaded to give up and are commonly acted upon by other people.

Discussion

Think of a time when you made an easy excuse not to take responsibility for your actions, e.g., it was someone else's fault, I missed the bus, my dog ate my homework.

Think of a time when you chose to take responsibility for your actions and demonstrated the willpower needed to succeed, e.g., I should have completed my homework on time, I should have left home earlier to catch the bus, I let the other person distract me.

For each of the above, determine which created a better circumstance where you took control of the outcome.

Having willpower and staying focused on what we want when we want it, by being true to our ideal Unique Signature, is as simple as it sounds. Part One gave us the mindset strategies to use in adopting and developing the required thinking and attitude, while Part Two gave us the strategies to recognise our intentions and values in order to follow through with our decisions and move forward with determination. Go back and revisit these if needed.

When we establish our purpose in life, our reason is driven and makes sense. People who accomplish this drive are able to withstand the effects of any setbacks they may encounter due to continuously moving forward, towards their ideal Unique Signature. Yet, many people who accomplish this are misunderstood and are sometimes referred to as cold blooded, arrogant and heartless because they do not waver from their decided plan of action. This criticism generally comes from those who are not taking responsibility for their actions and are envious of other's success.

Individual Activity

Have you ever criticised someone because they refused to waver from their decision or purpose to suit your needs?

Reflect on why you believe they did not change their mind or actions.

In retrospect, do you think that their purpose and plan of action was in order to achieve their Unique Signature?

Were they successful in what they wanted to achieve?

If we are accountable for everything we think, say, do, and are, we will consistently reach the goals required to accomplish our ideal Unique Signature.

Reaching Your Goal

Planning to reach a goal is not the same as actually reaching it. We may choose to follow the pathway towards reaching a goal, or the one that leads away from our goal. If we choose the latter, then the goal is no longer attainable.

Success is unavoidable if we remain focused on what we want. Reflecting again on when we first learned to walk, write our name or ride a bike, while we remained focused it was inevitable for the only possible outcome to be success. Failing indicates that we have given up, lost focus or not yet reached our goal. If we want to succeed, we must refuse to accept any circumstance that means not reaching our goal.

If we begin various projects without first completing one before starting the next, we may lose direction and drive towards reaching the desired outcome. We simply do not have the stamina to commit to so many projects. If we are unable to say 'no', we may take on more than we can manage. Week 12 addressed making the genuine decisions that will give us the greatest chance of reaching our desired goals. By being responsible and making genuine decisions that are true to our Unique Signature, we continue the forward momentum needed to remain on the pathway to succeed in reaching our goals.

> **'A dog that chases two rabbits goes hungry. Don't be the person who starts many things and finishes few.'**
> — Unknown

Weekly Task

Reflect on your vision board and the pathway you genuinely decided to accomplish from Week 16.

Determine this week if you are taking responsibility for the following strategies to reach your goal:

The time set aside to achieve this pathway.

The productive activities you have established to make this pathway a reality.

The abilities you trust within yourself to make this happen.

The attitude and habits you have adopted towards being committed to accomplishing this goal.

The decisions and actions you are being accountable for towards achieving this.

The results you are paying attention to as evidence of being in alignment with your ideal pathway.

Taking responsibility for any setback you may encounter.

Being persistent and remaining focused on your goals to accomplish this pathway.

For any strategies that require more work, revisit any weekly activities you believe are necessary to address this deficiency.

While completing this week's activity, be sure to stay true to your ideal Unique Signature. If we are not passionate about our chosen pathway, the chances of staying focused and taking purposeful action will prove limited, which is disadvantageous to moving towards our success.

Week 26

The Perfection Myth

We all have the unrealistic opinion that we must achieve everything we do to perfection, placing unnecessary pressure on ourselves and those around us. Most people who don't accomplish what they want in life are constantly influenced by their own or others' negative opinions and are easily persuaded to change their mind, often because they are conforming to the myth of being perfect. Our fear of not being perfect can destroy our imagination, innovation, ability to reason, and our efforts, which is disadvantageous towards achieving our Unique Signature.

The reality is, perfection is very subjective to the beholder. Anyone who thinks they are perfect has not yet experienced love or loss. However, if we must pursue the idea of perfection, creating our own perfection is creating our ideal circumstances by making and following our decisions without wavering. This will result in experiencing a life filled with perfection – our own perfection.

Discussion

Have you ever stopped doing what you enjoyed or begun doing what you disliked because of someone else's opinion?

Did that situation cost you peace of mind, joy, time, and/or money?

Have you ever imposed your opinion (idea of perfection) on someone's chosen pathway?

When we are unsure about any aspect of our life, it does not mean we are any less perfect than the next person. It is important to distinguish between asking for advice and being influenced by others' opinions. Asking for advice is completing our due diligence and remaining in control of our decisions and actions.

Thinking back to when we were young children, we had no hesitation in asking for assistance when we were unsure and needed help or guidance. As adults, we sometimes let our pride take over and decline help or refuse to ask for it when needed. It is ok to say 'I don't know how' or 'I need help' or 'I'm not confident about doing this on my own'. Admitting this does not mean we relinquish authority over our life and allow ourselves to be acted upon. Even people who have established themselves in esteemed positions constantly seek guidance and assistance without surrendering to others' opinions.

In 1916, Henry Ford sued the *Chicago Tribune* for writing he was 'an ignorant idealist', 'incapable of thought' and was 'not educated'. During the trial, the prosecutor pointed out that Ford was 'virtually illiterate' and asked a series of American trivia questions, to which Ford answered incorrectly, proving the paper was not at fault. Ford's response to these questions was, 'Now, will you kindly tell me why I should clutter up my mind with general knowledge for the purpose of being able to answer questions when I have people around me who can supply any knowledge I require?' Every person in the courtroom then realised this was the answer of an educated man, not an ignorant man.

Anyone who knows how to retrieve knowledge when needed and how to organise that knowledge into definite plans of action is educated (Napoleon Hill). Ford knew where to find knowledge when he needed it and had the wisdom to act upon it.

This grand example is of one of the most successful people the world has known, someone who shaped the industrial world. He was not perfect but he possessed enough wisdom and tenacity to be successful. Ford was just like everyone else who has a passion and acts on it.

> 'Whether you believe you can
> or whether you believe you can't,
> you're right.'
>
> — Henry Ford

What Success Means to You

Everyone loves a winner. In the 21st century, a 'winner' is generally defined by how much money they have in their bank account. However, money is only one indicator of success in a person's life. The successful person is the one who has abundance in the areas of their life that matter the most to their Unique Signature.

'Success' in the broadest sense can be applied to our career, lifestyle, material possessions, finances, spirituality, health, and mental wellbeing. However, the starting point of any success is desire. With desire, we open our mind to receiving and accepting the success we make for ourselves.

What our 'story of success' looks like depends on our mindset, the decisions we make, organised planning, deliberate actions, and persistence. These all contribute to the fundamental principles of success – quality and quantity. These help us determine whether we are consistently in alignment with our ideal Unique Signature and what course corrections are required to achieve success.

Quality of Success

Are we fulfilling our ideal Unique Signature in the most efficient manner possible, while keeping our personal success always in mind? When we experience success, feelings of pride, contentment and joy tell us we are in alignment and that continuing this pathway will inevitably result in greater success.

Quantity of Success

Are we adopting the correct habits to increase our personal success by developing our skills through practice and life experience? When we attain success, we benefit from any new knowledge and wisdom gained, which can later be applied towards further successes.

By continually attaining our desired quality and quantity of success, we avoid becoming disengaged, stagnant, or lacking in drive, making further successes impossible. By not attaining new skills or having new experiences in life, we deny ourselves our basic freedom to live our life to the fullest.

During each weekly activity, we have affirmed what we decide to accomplish while establishing the new habits required to make up for any drawbacks to our success. During Weeks 1 to 9, we affirmed and established the ideal mindset needed to achieve the successes we seek in our life. During Weeks 10 to 18, we affirmed and established our personal intentions for appropriate decision-making strategies to create our ideal circumstances in life. And in Weeks 19 to 25, we affirmed and established the type of actions that give us the skills necessary to know our own success.

When we feel our intentions, behaviours, habits, posture, decisions, and actions are in harmony, then we know that the quality and quantity of our success align with our Unique Signature.

Individual Activity

List the qualities and quantities of successful attributes you possess. Refer to your list of strengths from Week 1 and your list of what you want in life and who you want to be from Week 2 to assist you, then build on your list further.

Analyse your list and determine if you are meeting the desired quality and quantity of your success.

If not, what do you need to do to make your success a reality?

Thinking over the course of each weekly activity, reflect on whether you were inspired by the possibilities of creating your ideal Unique Signature while becoming the person you want to be. Have you struggled with the idea of seeing yourself in different circumstances from those you are in now?

If you have struggled, it may indicate you are not quite in alignment with your future ideal Unique Signature. It's ok to change your mind, just do so for what you want and be true to yourself with what you are seeking. The possibilities for achieving what you are capable of are endless.

Weekly Task

Write a short story about what your 'Story of Success' looks like to you.

Where do you live?

How is your health?

What qualifications do you have?

What is your occupation?

What type of car do you drive?

Are you going on a holiday soon?

Who is in your close circle of friends and family?

Are you at peace with yourself?

When you have finished, compare this to your vision board. Are there any notable differences? Truthfully ask yourself, 'Which representation is my true ideal Unique Signature?' and be determined to make it a reality.

'Success is not the key to happiness.
Happiness is the key to success.
If you love what you are doing,
you will be successful.'
—Albert Schweitzer

Week 27

Believe It Will Be

Our self-belief can produce better results when we are in harmony with our emotions, habits, decisions and actions. Perceiving ourselves as our Unique Signature *now* draws us closer to the reality of our ideal success story. When we concentrate on the concept of having what we desire, we experience joy and this elevates our drive, which authenticates our self-belief – 'it will be'.

Discussion

While completing each discussion, individual activity and weekly task, have you felt in harmony with your decisions and actions?

Have you used these feelings wisely to anticipate your next move?

Has there been any situation while participating in this course where your self-belief has been challenged?

Our self-belief may be challenged when we lack a well-defined purpose in our life. There is no chance of success if we do not have a purpose or a definite goal. Wanting something for nothing means we lack ambition to aim above the mediocre life we already have. When we don't have a definite goal, we tend to take a gamble on our life.

We do not believe in our chosen desire or in our strengths, and we are likely to abandon due diligence and sound decision-making. Believing in our Unique Signature gives us the confidence to constantly move forward to get what we want, no matter what.

Guessing instead of thinking, places our self-belief in doubt, whereas knowing and acting on instinct is believing in our ability to get what we want. If we think good things, we will attract good things.

> **'The world has the habit of making room for the person whose words and actions show that they know where they are going.'**
> — Napoleon Hill

Things Happen for a Reason

Everything happens for a reason. Is being in the right place at the right time by chance, or did we have the belief in our ability to be in the right place at the right time? In Week 14, we discussed how some people are perceived as lucky while others continually struggle through adversities. The latter create their own undesirable circumstances by not acting because they do not believe anything will change. In Week 19, we explored how to create the ideal circumstances to move forward to where we want to be, through inspired thought and by acting upon our thoughts.

Individual Activity

Since beginning this course of activities, have you changed the way you react when an opportunity presents itself?

Do you delay, second-guess or doubt yourself? Or do you act swiftly with confidence and self-belief?

Confidence and self-belief place people in the right place at the right time. Acting upon an inspired thought creates positive circumstances in a person's life. That is why things 'happen for a reason'.

Weekly Task

Think back to last week's task. Choose one affirmation that is in alignment with your success story and your vision board.

Concentrate this week on the intentions, decisions and actions needed to create the ideal circumstances that will place you in the right place at the right time to make your affirmation a reality.

Being authentic in our positive intentions helps us attract beneficial experiences into our life. If we don't like or feel good about our current circumstances, only we can take responsibility for changing our circumstances into what we desire, thus influencing what happens in our life now and in the future.

Remember:
Everything happens for a reason,
and that reason is
YOU!

— S.T.

Week 28

The Ideal You

Having a desire and seeking what we want is not something poisonous or selfish, it is serving our ideal Unique Signature so that we are not a burden to ourselves or anyone else. To maintain our commitment towards our Unique Signature, we require continuous reflection on the forward, idle and backward directions that we experience in the pursuit of our success. This does not mean we need to analyse every small decision we make or the actions we take, which would be unhealthy and cause us unnecessary stress. Rather, we need to set aside time to reflect, weekly, fortnightly or monthly.

It's your life; you choose.

By asking ourselves some simple questions about our attitude towards our career, lifestyle, love, relationships, material possessions, finances, spirituality, health, and mental wellbeing, we are able to make a solid assessment and ascertain what is and is not in alignment with our ideal Unique Signature.

Is my attitude and intention in harmony with my Unique Signature?

Have I attained the goal that was my objective for this week/month/year?

Have I permitted fear, limiting beliefs, self-doubt, and procrastination to decrease my efficiency, and if so, in what way?

Have I been open-minded to observing opportunities and new experiences?

Have I reached decisions promptly by carrying out due diligence?

Have I dissipated any of my energy through lack of direction, or have I utilised my energy with effort, persistence and deliberate action?

Have my conversations been shallow and meaningless or have they been purposeful and passionate?

Have any of my habits resulted in time wasting and completing less purposeful activities?

Have my opinions and decisions been based on guesswork, or on accurate analysis and thought?

Have I followed the habit of budgeting my time towards success?

How much of my time have I devoted to self-education to benefit my Unique Signature?

How many challenging decisions have I made to place myself outside my comfort zone, compared to safe decisions?

Have I continued to adopt new habits that will give me control over my life?

Have I chosen the correct pathway that will bring me joy and reflect my ideal Unique Signature?

What is my present appraisal on the fundamental principles of success (quality and quantity)?

The most important step from now is to acknowledge that 'We don't need to see the entire staircase, we just need to take the first step' (Martin Luther King Jr). When walking or driving, we never know what is around the next corner. But we have to travel that distance to get to where we want to go. If we stop the car and refuse to move further, we will become stranded in a location that may not suit what we want or where we want to be. Our life is no different from this analogy.

> **'The journey of a thousand miles begins with a single step.'**
>
> — Lao Tzu

Weekly Task

Over this week, answer every question for each area of your life with deliberate thought and honesty. Keep your answers in a safe place.

Choose an area of your life that is not currently in alignment with your Unique Signature.

Go through every weekly activity and task of this course and select the appropriate methods that will be useful for you to accomplish your desired circumstances.

Pay special attention to designing and organising a deliberate plan to create the specific results you want. Ensure you give yourself a realistic time frame for each achievement.

Reflect weekly on your progress and make any course corrections, such as a shift in your mindset, decisions or actions that will achieve the positive outcomes you seek.

When you feel ready, refer to the answers from this weekly task and reflect on any other areas of your life that are not in alignment with your Unique Signature.

Only you have the authority to establish your ideal Unique Signature. Remember to take your time, without floundering or procrastinating, to accomplish every desire that brings you joy. After each accomplishment, take some time to celebrate then move forward with refreshed effort and enthusiasm to bring about the next reality for your ideal Unique Signature.

Over the past 28 weeks, we have explored and applied activities to enhance our self-belief towards achieving our ideal Unique Signature and success. All aspects of our ideal Unique Signature are equally important and essential for maintaining our self-belief and joy in our chosen ideal lifestyle.

Epilogue

As our mind is our biggest asset to achieve our ideal life, how we think from this moment forward will forge and shape our attitude and posture towards who we will remain and who we will become.

As we maintain our purpose, intentions and values to accomplish whatever we desire in our ideal life, our choices from this moment forward will forge and shape what will continue to be and what will begin anew.

And as we decide what actions we need to take to consistently develop our experience and wisdom, what we do from this moment forward will forge and shape the circumstances we experience and the consequences of these will influence our future decisions.

Whatever we desire from this moment forward requires a driven mindset, decisions with purpose and actions with deliberate effort to succeed.

And whatever we desire from this moment forward should be in alignment with our expectations of what our ideal Unique Signature truly looks like, by experiencing the joy that is naturally instilled within us.

Now go forward with inspiration, knowing you have the ability and self-belief to make it happen. Your Unique Signature is counting on it.

'Inspiration is the greatest gift
because it opens your life
to many new possibilities.'
— Bernie Siegel

References

Broderick, P. & Blewitt, P. (2014) *The Life Span: Human Development for Helping Professionals* (4thed.). USA: Pearson.

Brown, D. (2011) *The Experiment: The Secret of Luck*. S1, Ep4. SBS. (viewed 12 December 2013)

Byrne, R. (2006) *The Secret*. Oregon: Atria Books.

Canniford, L. & Fox-Young, S. (2013). 'Learning and assessing competence in reflective practice: Student evaluation of the relative value of aspects of an integrated, interactive reflective practice syllabus.' *Collegian*. 22(3), 291-297. Retrieved from http://learnjcu.jcu.edu.au

Domeyko Rowland, M. (1994) *Absolute Happiness - The Whole Untold Story - The Way to a Life of Complete Fulfilment*. Australia: Self Communications.

Dyer, W. (2013) *I Can See Clearly Now*. California: Hay House.

Ellis, A. & Dryden, W. (1997) *The Practice of Rational Emotive Behaviour Therapy* (2nded.). New York, US: Springer.

Enticott, J. Meadows, G. Shawyer, F. Inder, B. & Patten, S (2016) 'Mental disorders and distress: Associations with demographics, remoteness and socioeconomic deprivation of area of residence across Australia.' *Australian & New Zealand Journal of Psychiatry*. 50(12), 1169-1179. doi: 10.1177/0004867415615948

Geldard, D. & Geldard, K. (2012) *Basic Personal Counselling: A Training Manual for Counsellors* (7thed.). Frenchs Forest, NSW: Pearson.

Hicks, E & J (2008) *The Law of Attraction*. California: Hay House.

Hill, N. (2009) *Think and Grow Rich*. United Kingdom: Capstone Publishing Ltd.

Kiyosaki, R. (2011) *Cashflow Quadrant - Guide to Financial Freedom: Rich Dad's Guide to Financial Freedom*. Scottsdale: Plata Publishing.

Parrish, D. & Crookes, K. (2013). 'Designing and implementing reflective practice programs – Key principles and considerations.' *Nurse Education in Practice*. 14, 265-270. Retrieved from http://learnjcu.jcu.edu.au

Waitley, Dr D. (1986) *The Psychology of Winning*. New York: Penguin Publishing Group.

Warren, J. (01/2012) 'Mobile mind mapping: Using mobile technology to enhance rational emotive behaviour therapy.' *Journal of Mental Health Counselling*. 34(1), 72-81. Retrieved from http://learnjcu.jcu.edu.au

www.ingramcontent.com/pod-product-compliance
Lightning Source LLC
Chambersburg PA
CBHW071624080526
44588CB00010B/1255